IDIOT'S GUIDES®

AS EASY AS IT GETS!

Grilling

by Chef Thomas N. England

ALPHA

A member of Penguin Random House LLC

ALPHA BOOKS

Published by A member of Penguin Random House LLC

Penguin Random House LLC, 375 Hudson Street, New York, New York 10014, USA · Penguin Random House LLC (Canada), 90 Eglinton Avenue East, Suite 700, Toronto, Ontario M4P 2Y3, Canada (a division of Pearson Penguin Canada Inc.) · Penguin Books Ltd., 80 Strand, London WC2R 0RL, England · Penguin Ireland, 25 St. Stephen's Green, Dublin 2, Ireland (a division of Penguin Books Ltd.) · Penguin Random House LLC (Australia), 250 Camberwell Road, Camberwell, Victoria 3124, Australia (a division of Pearson Australia Group Pty. Ltd.) · Penguin Books India Pvt. Ltd., 11 Community Centre, Panchsheel Park, New Delhi—110 017, India · Penguin Random House LLC (NZ), 67 Apollo Drive, Rosedale, North Shore, Auckland 1311, New Zealand (a division of Pearson New Zealand Ltd.) · Penguin Books (South Africa) (Pty.) Ltd., 24 Sturdee Avenue, Rosebank, Johannesburg 2196, South Africa · Penguin Books Ltd., Registered Offices: 80 Strand, London WC2R 0RL, England

002-254072-May2016

IDIOT'S GUIDES and Design are trademarks of Penguin Random House LLC

International Standard Book Number: 978-1-61564-456-8
Library of Congress Catalog Card Number: 2013952989

17 16 15   8 7 6 5 4 3 2

Interpretation of the printing code: The rightmost number of the first series of numbers is the year of the book's printing; the rightmost number of the second series of numbers is the number of the book's printing. For example, a printing code of 13-1 shows that the first printing occurred in 2013.

Printed in China

Publisher: Mike Sanders
Executive Managing Editor: Billy Fields
Executive Acquisitions Editor: Lori Cates Hand
Development Editor: Kayla Dugger
Production Editor: Jana M. Stefanciosa

Senior Designer: Rebecca Batchelor
Indexer: Celia McCoy
Layout: Ayanna Lacey
Proofreader: Jaime Julian Wagner
Photographer: Michael Hickey
archive.michaelhickeyphotography.com

Contents

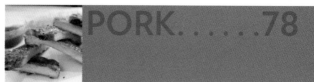

VEGETABLES 206

FRUIT . . . 244

BREAD/CHEESE ..266

DESSERTS
. . . . 284

Introduction

For many, grilling out is a time that's associated with friends and family gathered around in the backyard for an afternoon of leisure. It's a picture of simpler times, and this idyllic scene is what brings many to the grill. But do you find yourself tensing up with anxiety when you have to cook on a grill? Do your friends offer to cook when you invite them over to cook out? Then this book is for you.

I start by teaching you about the various types of grills and how to choose the best one for your purpose. You then get a rundown of all the other tools you need to make the grilling easy and fun. I next give you a collection of recipes for spices and sauces that will take your grilled foods from good to great. Finally, you get step-by-step recipes and instructions for grilling your favorite meats, poultry, seafood, fruits and vegetables, and more.

A couple of things make the recipes in the book unique. With each recipe, I include a list of all the utensils and equipment that you need. This will help you organize everything before you get outside and realize you need to run in and out to get additional items. And I've developed the recipes so that each step of the cooking process includes a picture. Sometimes new techniques can be confusing, so these pictures help to clarify the processes.

Except for the fruits and vegetables (which are in alphabetical order), I've also organized the recipes by popularity. The recipe that would be used most often is listed first, while the final recipe of each chapter tends to be one that's more advanced and great to work toward. Each chapter also includes sidebars. These items can provide tips for making the recipe, tell a story about the recipe, and give more information to those interested in the deeper meaning of the food being made.

Once you're at the grill and master it, it becomes a belief system, and you become a grilling addict. Continue reading, and you'll be on your way to that grilling addiction.

Acknowledgments

There are several people I would like to thank; without their guidance, help, and encouragement, this book would not have been possible.

Like many chefs, my life has not always been in the kitchen. It was during difficult transitional times that I found myself comforted in a busy restaurant. I would like to thank the teachers and advisors at the University of Evansville for encouraging my love for the business. It's that encouragement that ultimately made the connections for this book.

Writing this book was a team effort. The initial manuscript was reviewed by Carolyn Doyle. Without her steady eye, the book would be a collection of French restaurant terms. Through the countless hours, the publisher's editorial and art teams made my writing look effortless. And the students and faculty of Ivy Tech Community College were a huge help. They did all the recipe testing and helped prepare all the food for the pictures. Special acknowledgment is due to Carolyn Doyle, Anne McNevin, and Paul Vida for their hard work for the photo shoots.

And for always encouraging me through everything I do, special acknowledgment is due to Karen Mangia, Joanna England, and Tony England. Thank you for helping me grow as a person every day.

GRILLING ESSENTIALS

Basic Grilling Techniques

The Direct-Heat Method

The direct-heat grilling technique is what most people start out using when they learn to grill. Direct heat uses a heat source that's directly below the item being cooked. The direct heat helps develop the brown caramelization in the foods. Not only does this browning add eye appeal, it also delivers a more intense flavor.

What to Cook with Direct Heat

The direct-heat method is ideal for foods that take less than 20 minutes to cook. Foods that are best suited for direct heat are the following:

- Fish fillets
- Thinner, tender cuts of meat, such as steaks, hamburgers, and chops
- Kebabs
- Sausages and hot dogs
- Fruits and vegetables

All recipes in this book list the preheat temperature for your grill. With the direct-heat cooking method, this is listed as a low to high range. To determine how hot the grill is, use the following chart.

DETERMINING THE GRILL TEMPERATURE

Temperature	How Long You Can Hold Your Hand About 5 Inches (12.75 cm) Above the Grate
Low heat	6 or more seconds
Medium heat	4 to 5 seconds
Medium-high heat	3 to 4 seconds
High heat	Less than 3 seconds

How to Cook with the Direct-Heat Method

When grilling using the direct-heat cooking method, follow these steps:

For a **gas grill,** bring the heat up by turning all burners on and closing the lid for 15 minutes. After that, turn the temperature down to the appropriate level for the recipe.

For a **charcoal grill,** bring up the heat by spreading the coals in the grill so they're sloped more on one end than the other. This allows you to have a variety of temperatures across the grill.

Once the grill grate is hot, scrub it with a wire brush to get off any accumulation of burned-on food residue.

Oil an old cloth with vegetable oil. Roll it up into a tight roll and, using a long pair of tongs, wipe off the hot grate. This removes any leftover soot that can make the food taste bitter.

Season food to be cooked with kosher or sea salt.

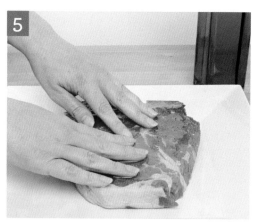

Oil food. By oiling after seasoning, you avoid seasoning running off food as it cooks.

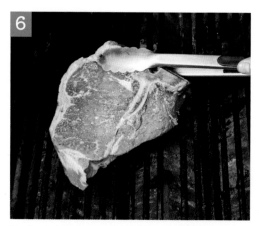

Put food directly over the heat source. This is done to develop the brown caramelization and grill hash marks. With thicker cuts, you should move food to a cooler part of the grill to finish cooking all the way through.

MAILLARD REACTION

The Maillard reaction is a principle that says in the absence of water, sugars combine with acids to produce a new flavor. The process of adding salt and putting the food on direct heat is used to create the Maillard reaction. The salt absorbs any water still on the exterior of the food, and the oil prevents moisture from the air from getting to the food. The heat then develops the sugars in the food to create the reaction. You can't get this kind of flavor development from iodized salt because it doesn't absorb moisture.

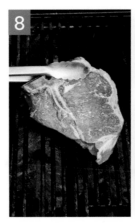

Keep the lid off the grill as you cook. Putting the lid on when using direct heat causes the flame to lose oxygen, which in turn lowers the temperature. However, if you're grilling in the middle of winter or when it's raining, you can put the lid on—just make sure all the vents are open so the flame gets enough oxygen to stay hot.

To ensure food is evenly cooked, turn it over once during the cooking process.

TYPES OF SALT

Type of Salt	Description
Fleur de sel	Sea salt harvested from evaporating ponds as the salt forms on the top of the water. You use this salt on foods after they've been cooked.
Himalayan salt	These salts are mined from deposits in Pakistan and are said to be the purest form of salt. Himalayan salts are often counterfeited by companies that add red color to the salt. Finer grinds are great for general use.
Hawaiian sea salt	These salts can be either pink or black—pink because of the red-clay soils around the island, and black because of volcanic ash. This salt is ideal for pork and seafood.
Kosher salt	So named because it's used in kosher meat preparation, kosher salt is a good all-purpose salt; however, not all kosher salt is certified kosher. It can come from the earth or the sea, dissolves easily, and has a looser cell structure than table salt.
Table salt	Mined salt, mostly from New York, that's most often used in salt shakers. Other chemicals, such as iodine and anti-caking agents, are often added to it. Table salt is very dense and good for baking applications; however, it should rarely be used for meat preparation.

The Indirect-Heat Method

As people begin to branch out and try to grill more things, they turn to the indirect-heat cooking method. For this method, there's no heat directly under the food; instead, the food is cooked by the heat around it. The indirect-heat method helps the food develop nuanced flavors that can't be created using the faster direct-heat cooking method.

What to Cook with Indirect Heat

This cooking technique is suited for grilling foods that take longer than 20 minutes to cook—in other words, larger items. These could include the following:

- Beef tenderloin
- Prime rib
- Beef short rib
- Pork roast
- Leg of lamb
- Whole poultry
- Whole fish

All the recipes in this book list the preheat temperature for your grill. With the indirect-heat cooking method, this is listed as an exact temperature. Many grills come with a thermometer in the lid, but use an in-oven thermometer to check the accuracy of the grill.

How to Cook with the Indirect-Heat Method

When grilling using the indirect-heat cooking method, follow these steps:

For a **gas grill,** bring up the heat by turning all burners on and closing the lid for 15 minutes. After that, turn the middle burner off, adjust the temperature down to the appropriate level for the recipe, and place a disposable aluminum roasting pan under the middle of the grate.

For a **charcoal grill,** bring up the heat by spreading the coals in the grill so they're arranged around a disposable aluminum roasting pan; this allows the heat to radiate around the product being cooked. The pan also collects any juices from meat, which can later be used in a sauce.

Scrub the grate with a wire brush to get off any accumulation of food residue.

Oil an old cloth with vegetable oil. Roll it up into a tight roll and, using a long pair of tongs, wipe off the hot grate. This removes any leftover soot that can make food taste bitter.

Season food to be cooked with kosher or sea salt.

Oil food. By oiling after seasoning, you avoid seasoning running off food as it cooks.

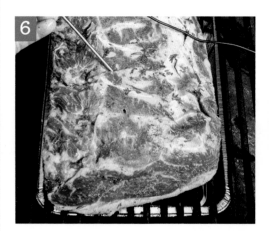

Place food over the drip pan.

Keep the lid on the grill as you cook. Opening the lid too much during indirect-heat cooking makes the grill lose heat and moisture, which increases cooking time and could make your food drier.

For a **gas grill,** control the heat by turning the flame up or down on the burners that aren't directly under item being cooked.

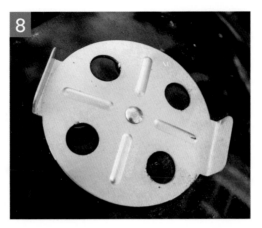

For a **charcoal grill,** control the heat by opening and closing the vents at the top or bottom of the grill. The more the vents are open at the bottom of the grill, the more oxygen can get to the coals to produce heat. Opening the top vent creates a draw through the grill; this pulls oxygen into the grill from the bottom vents, producing a higher heat.

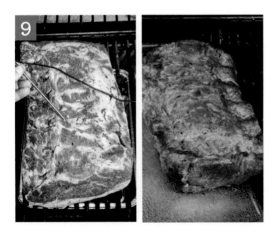

To ensure food is evenly cooked, turn it over once during the cooking process.

Smoking

Grill cooks who become addicted to outdoor cooking tend to graduate to smoking foods, as it's how you truly develop barbecue. This process demands good control over the heat, as well as nuances you can achieve with smoldering woods. Smoking uses indirect heat, low temperatures, and long time periods.

The smoking technique I explain in this section is the hot smoking technique. You can do this on a charcoal or gas grill, but there are many specialized smokers developed for this specific process.

What to Cook with Smoking

Hot smoking is best suited for large, tough cuts of meat, including the following:

- Beef brisket
- Pork butt (shoulder) for pulled or chopped pork
- Whole pigs

GRILLING TRIVIA

Barbecue is not a verb; rather, it's food developed through the smoking process. You can invite people over to grill; you can't invite them over to barbecue. However, you can invite people over to eat barbecue, or meats that had been cooked for a long time with some smoke.

How to Smoke Food

When using the smoking method, follow these steps:

Bring up the heat and clean the grill using the same steps as in the indirect-heat cooking method.

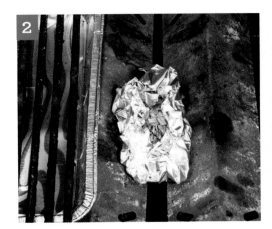

Place item in the grill that will produce the smoke, such as a wood log, wood chunks, or wood shavings.

To produce the low temperatures for anywhere from 3 to 24 hours with a charcoal grill, put the unlit charcoal around the drip pan and then place just eight pieces of lit charcoal on top. The lit charcoal will slowly light the unlit coals, allowing you to go without adding charcoal for several hours.

Season food to be cooked with kosher or sea salt and other seasonings as recommended. This often includes larger amounts of salt and sugars. These balance the flavor of the smoke and help to contain the growth of bacteria on food. Because you want to get the smoke to penetrate into food, don't oil it.

Place food over the drip pan with the side that has the most fat on the bottom; otherwise, oil from fat will push off seasonings as it cooks.

Keep the lid closed during the smoking process, unless you have to add more coals to maintain the temperature. The combination of smoke and the lack of oxygen helps to develop a red smoke ring around the outside of meat, which aficionados look for as a sign of good barbecue.

CHEF'S TIP

Smoke penetrates into the meat only about ⅛ inch (.25 cm). To get great flavor and really maximize the smoke flavor, start with very cold meat. The hot smoke is attracted to moisture, so putting cold meat into a hot smoker will cause it to sweat. The smoke will then go to that condensation and concentrate onto the meat as the water evaporates, giving you the deeper smoky flavor you want.

GRILLING FOOD SAFETY

The last thing you want to serve guests at a party is a foodborne illness. Follow these simple safety guidelines when grilling:

- Never leave meat and perishables out more than two hours.

- Never partially cook meats and think you can go back and cook them more later.

- Keep hot foods above 140°F (60°C) while you're serving them.

- Keep cold foods below 40°F (4°C) while you're serving them.

- Never put cooked foods on the same plate that they were on when they were uncooked. For example, the tray that held those raw steaks you brought out to the grill is *not* the same tray the steaks should be on for the return trip (unless you've washed, rinsed, and sanitized it in the meantime).

- Cook foods to the internal temperature recommended by the government's recommendations. All the recipes in the book are written to reflect the temperatures recommended by the U.S. Food and Drug Administration.

WOOD FOR SMOKING

Wood Type	Smoke Qualities	Best Suited For
Apple	Slightly sweet, fruity character	Fruits, game birds, and pork
Cherry	Slightly sweet, mild smoke; gives a reddish smoke color	All meats
Hickory	Sweet, strong smoke flavor	Pork and beef
Maple	Mild smoke	Poultry
Mesquite	Strong earthy flavor	Beef and game
Oak	Mild smoke flavor; very little bitterness	Pork and poultry
Pecan	Sweet, mild smoke flavor	Poultry, chicken, fish, and cheese

Grills

Gas Grills

Gas grills offer the convenience of being able to just turn a knob to control the heat. You don't have to plan out how long it will take to heat up the charcoal, how you need to layer it in the grill, or how you need to adjust vents to control the heat. Gas grills come in a wide range of prices—from $50 for a tabletop version to $10,000 for one that has your name spelled out in the grate and will talk to you. So how much you spend is based on what you really need and want from it. The following are some things you should consider when purchasing a gas grill.

Construction: Gas grills made from heavy metals are the best. The heavy metals hold their heat the longest, so you can maintain an even heat throughout the inside of the grill. However, if you just plan on doing direct-heat cooking during good weather, this isn't important.

Number of burners: The number of burners in a gas grill can vary greatly. If you're doing small amounts of grilling and using only the direct-heat method, you can buy a gas grill with one burner. If you're going to grill more than six burgers at a time, you need something bigger. It's important to note that for indirect-heat cooking, you need at least three burners.

BTUs (British Thermal Units): This is the measure of how much heat is put out by the burners—the larger the number of BTUs, the more heat that can be produced. This is important if you want to do high-heat direct cooking or indirect cooking above 350°F (177°C).

Heavy grates: When it comes to grates on a gas grill, you want something made from heavy metal, with tines that are close together. If they're too thin and light, they'll warp under high heat. If the tines are too far apart, the food will fall through into the fire. In an ideal world, look for grates made of cast iron with tines that are ½ inch (1.25 cm) apart. If the gas grill doesn't come like this, see if you can buy a grate that size to upgrade it.

Side burners: A side burner is like a regular stove burner. These are nice if you plan to cook other stovetop items while grilling, because they can save you from needing to cook anything inside.

Rotisserie: Many gas grills today come equipped with a rotisserie, which is nice if you want to cook a whole chicken. Be sure to see how much clearance space these have—some are so small, you would be lucky to be able to put the smallest chicken on and still allow it to rotate.

Pull-out drip tray: Most foods drip juices as they cook, so good-quality gas grills have trays under the grates to catch anything that isn't vaporized as it falls. You can then empty the tray out periodically. If you're a heavy grill user and you don't have one of these trays, you run the risk of having grease accumulate on the bottom of the grill, which can lead to a grease fire.

Charcoal Grills

Charcoal grills offer a lot in the way of flavor, as the burning charcoal or wood produces flavors that can enhance the food. But cooking with charcoal means a lot more planning needs to go into the process (see the "Working with Charcoal" section). With charcoal grills, you also need to learn more about how to control the temperature of the grill. This comes with practice and knowing the charcoal or woods you're working with. Here are some things to consider when looking to buy a charcoal grill.

Construction: Charcoal grills made from materials that hold their heat are ideal, because they let you maintain an even heat throughout the inside of them. In order to hold their heat, the lid and all the parts should fit tightly together so they don't allow in unwanted oxygen during low-temperature cooking. Also, look for vents in the top and bottom that are easily adjustable to control the temperature. If you just plan on doing direct-heat cooking during good weather, this type of construction isn't important.

Heavy grates: Like gas grills, the grates on charcoal grills should be made from a heavy metal such as cast iron, with tines that are about ½ inch (1.25 cm) apart. Grilling is far easier when you don't have to worry about the grates warping or being too wide and allowing food to fall through. If you like a charcoal grill that doesn't come this way, you can always see if grates are available to swap in for the ones that come standard.

Access to coals: With longer cooking times, you often need to add more coals. If you're going to smoke foods or use other long-cooking techniques, look for a charcoal grill that allows you to add new coals without opening the lid where the food is cooking.

Most Common Charcoal Grill Brands

The Big Green Egg brands itself as "the ultimate grilling experience," and it truly does offer everything you need in a charcoal grill. Big Green Egg charcoal grills are made of ceramics that hold their temperature very well, with grates that are heavy and narrow, and have accessories that can change from direct heat to indirect heat in seconds. The vents and shape of the egg make it easy to adjust temperature quickly from low heat to high heat.

Weber grills are also versatile. Their shape makes the radiation of heat around the inside of the grill consistent, and there are many accessories available to enable you to adapt the grill for different techniques, such as grates that have hinged sides so you can add wood chips for smoking or more coals for longer cooking with indirect heat.

Working with Charcoal

When lighting charcoal, never use lighter fluid. It gives off flavors that will carry onto the foods. Use a chimney to heat coals and then add the hot coals to your grill.

The types of charcoal on the market seem to have exploded in the past few years. The following are the most commonly used types of charcoal:

Briquettes are the most common type of charcoal and are reliable and easy to use. These were developed originally as a way to use boxes and pallets from manufacturing facilities. These items are ground and compacted into briquettes, taking waste out of the waste stream. Many companies also add chemicals to the briquettes to help them burn longer and more consistently.

Hardwood charcoal is charcoal made specifically from woods traditionally used for cooking. These tend to produce a better flavor in foods than briquettes. Quality hardwood charcoal should be somewhat consistent in size, with the absence of planks of charcoal. Planks will sometimes be in a bag of charcoal because the company is making the charcoal from scrap woods in a wood mill. It's assumed that the planks aren't from treated wood, but be leery of the source.

Infrared Grills

Infrared grills are propane or gas grills with special heat collecting and distribution systems. They take the heat from the burners and collect it onto a panel that radiates the heat up to what is cooking. As a result, the food cooks more quickly because the heat is directed intensely on it and not just around it, as with traditional grills. It also means it can use less gas to accomplish superior results.

What's a bit different is how the grates are constructed. The grates are where the traditional convection heat is changed to radiant heat, so look for efficiency ratings of 65 and above. Also, consider what material the radiant is made from. It should be a combination of stainless steel and ceramics.

The following are some of the qualities you should look for that are the same as with a traditional gas grill.

Number of burners: Look for grills that have at least three burners so you can do indirect-heat cooking.

BTUs: As with other grills, the higher the BTUs, the more heat that can be produced. In this case, you won't need as many BTUs as with a traditional gas grill to achieve the same results with searing. But if you're doing indirect-heat cooking, you'll still need higher BTUs.

Side burners: Side burners are nice to have to cook things off to the side while also cooking on the grill.

Rotisserie: Rotisseries are available for infrared grills and produce great results for browning and flavoring. Most often they are a separate burner attached to the back of the grill.

Pull-out drip tray: As with other gas grills, pull-out drip trays are important. You'll still get some liquids dripping down, so having a tray that collects these makes it easy to discard.

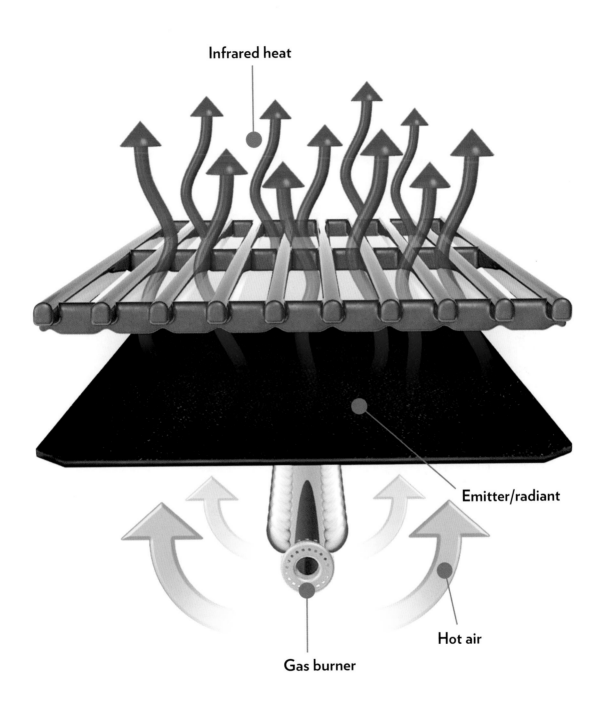

Infrared heat

Emitter/radiant

Hot air

Gas burner

Image © Char-Broil, LLC. Used with permission.

Smokers

Smokers are developed specifically to cook products low and slow with the addition of smoke. You can find a large variety of these, including charcoal, gas, and even electric. Most are not suited to direct-heat cooking. When shopping for a smoker, the following are a few qualities you should look for.

Smoke delivery: Smoking units can deliver smoke in many different ways, including having logs that smolder in a big box or pellets that are automatically dropped on a timer. Whichever way you choose, make sure you understand how the system works and the amount of time and effort each takes.

Size: The size of the area where the food goes varies dramatically from one smoker to the next, so be sure you know the size of the food items you want to cook. For example, if you want to smoke a turkey for Thanksgiving, make sure you know how wide that bird is so you can get a smoker big enough to fit it.

Heating control capacity: In smoking, you want to go up to 250°F (120°C) and maintain an even temperature for a long time. Therefore, look for smokers that have the ability to read and control temperatures.

Construction: Like with other grills, look for materials that hold heat and are able to withstand rain and cold.

Cold smoke: If you plan on cold smoking anything, look for units that also have refrigeration included.

TYPES OF WOOD FOR SMOKING

Wood	Qualities
Acacia	Earthy flavor; burns hot
Alder	Delicate flavor
Apple	Mild and fruity
Cherry	Mild; leaves a dark color on the exterior of meats
Grapevines	Aromatic with mild fruity flavor
Hickory	Strong flavors; best mixed with apple or oak
Lilac	Light smoke flavor with a hint of floral
Maple	Aromatic
Mesquite	Very strong earthy flavor; burns very hot
Oak	Mild and nutty
Pecan	Sweet and spicy
Walnut	Very smoky flavor with bitter qualities; best mixed with other woods

Grilling Tools

When grilling, having a few particular tools can make life easier. You don't need to go out and buy some über-expensive tools set in a nice case; a few simple things are all you need, and most of them are probably items you already have in your kitchen.

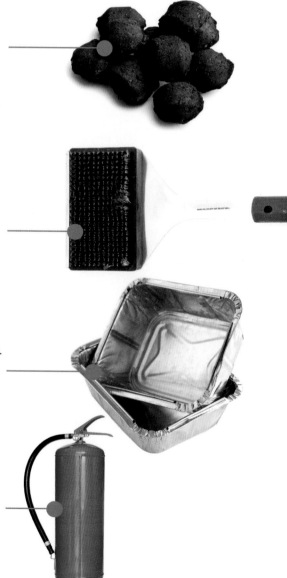

Charcoal: To cook and impart flavor to the food. Look for high-quality lump charcoal for high heat and long burning.

Chimney starter: To light charcoal. Look for a capacity that's larger, as new charcoals aren't consistent and may be too large and chunky for some.

Cleaning brush: To scrub the grill before and after each use. Look for sturdy metal bristles and a long handle.

Disposable foil pans: To collect the juices from meats being cooked using the indirect-heat cooking. Use a pan that's small enough to fit down into the center of the grill and allows the heat source to rise around it.

Fire extinguisher: To douse grill fires. Don't overlook this; you never know what might catch fire unexpectedly. Fire safety experts recommend you have a fire extinguisher near each cooking area in the household—this includes the outdoor grill.

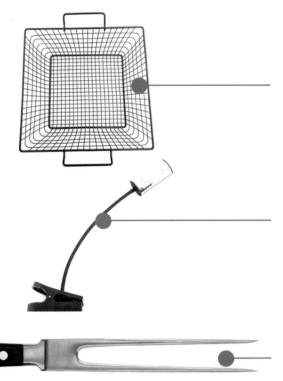

Grill basket: To grill items that are small enough to fall through the grate.

Hand garden trowel: To move coals around easily to get them adjusted. A metal trowel is great to have when working with charcoal.

Light: To aid you when grilling out at night. If you plan to do a lot of night grilling, it's an absolute necessity. Look for an LED light that has a clip to attach it to the grill and that provides true white light.

Meat fork: To pick up food. It should come to a point at the end and have a taper to enable you to pick up larger cuts of meat.

Meat thermometer: To keep track of the temperature of the food. This is the single most important item in the grilling toolkit. The thermometer should go from a minimum of 32°F to 212°F (0°C to 100°C) to cover a wide range of food temperatures.

Offset spatula: To turn ground meat and fish to keep them from falling apart. You can use a short-handled one, as long-handled versions are often harder to use and can result in foods such as fish falling apart from rough handling.

Oil cloth: To wipe down the grate before each use.

Rack lifter: To help you lift the hot grates out of the grill.

Sauce brush (mop): To baste your foods. The brush should be made of a heat-resistant material, such as boar bristle.

Silicone gloves: To lift hot grates. These withstand higher temperatures than hot pads and can be used anytime hot pads are called for in a recipe.

Skewers: To grill kebabs. When grilling kebabs, you need skewers that are flat and wide; this allows the skewers to be turned without spinning the food on it.

Squirt bottle: To help put out flames and add moisture to the air in the grill. You can also use a squirt gun or a cup of water.

Temperature regulator: To maintain temperatures when you're cooking with indirect heat on charcoal grills. There are several brands of regulators on the market.

Tongs: To pick up food. Look for tongs with a long reach that are made of metal and have a firm spring.

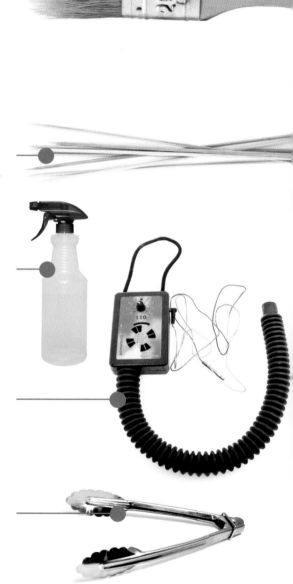

CONTROLLING THE FLAME—SAFELY

Controlling the flame of the grill is what grilling is all about, so be sure to do it in a safe manner. Follow these basic safety guidelines:

- Never use a grill indoors (including tents). They produce toxic fumes that can be deadly.

- Follow the manufacturer's guidelines for the grill you're using.

- Check the materials in the grill annually to ensure they're working properly.

- Never allow children within 3 feet of the grill.

- Make sure the grill is at least 10 feet away from any combustible material.

- Don't wear loose-fitting clothing or anything that could get caught on the grill.

- Never leave the grill unattended.

- Clean out the drip tray regularly.

- Keep a fire extinguisher within 10 feet of the grill.

- Don't spray pan spray over or near a lit grill.

- Never add lighter fluid to coals that are already lit.

Seasonings and Condiments

Sauces

Sauces are an important part of the history of barbecue. They used to be a way to help preserve the meats that were being cooked, because the salts and acids help control bacteria. Today, we add them by tradition but have altered them to make the sauces accent the flavors of meat better. Ultimately, it's about the flavor of the food that the sauce is being put onto—the flavors of the sauces shouldn't overpower the main food items.

In general, any of the sauces can be held in the refrigerator for 10 days, unless otherwise stated.

Alabama Barbecue Sauce

Yield: about 3½ cups	Prep time: 20 minutes

2 cups mayon-
naise

1 cup apple cider
vinegar

2 TB. lemon juice

3 TB. black
pepper

1 tsp. kosher salt

½ tsp. cayenne

1. In a small mixing bowl, combine mayonnaise, apple cider vinegar, lemon juice, black pepper, kosher salt, and cayenne.

2. Pour into an airtight container and store covered in the refrigerator. Allow sauce to refrigerate for at least 8 hours before using.

Bourbon Glaze

Yield: about 1 cup	Prep time: 10 minutes

4 TB. Dijon
mustard

3 TB. light brown
sugar

1 TB. molasses

1 TB. Worcester-
shire sauce

1 TB. orange juice

6 TB. bourbon

1. In a small mixing bowl, combine Dijon mustard, light brown sugar, molasses, Worcestershire sauce, orange juice, and bourbon.

2. Use immediately, or pour into an airtight container and store covered in the refrigerator until ready to use.

Carolina Barbecue Sauce

Yield: about 2 ¾ cups

Prep time: 30 minutes

Cook time: 10 minutes

1 cup prepared yellow mustard

½ cup granulated sugar

¼ cup light brown sugar

¾ cup cider vinegar

¼ cup water

2 TB. chili powder

1 tsp. black pepper

1 tsp. white pepper

¼ tsp. cayenne

½ tsp. soy sauce

2 TB. butter

1 TB. liquid smoke (hickory flavoring)

1. In a small mixing bowl, combine prepared yellow mustard, granulated sugar, light brown sugar, cider vinegar, water, chili powder, black pepper, white pepper, and cayenne.

2. In a small saucepan over medium heat, pour mixture, and simmer for 30 minutes.

3. Add soy sauce, butter, and liquid smoke, stir to combine, and simmer for 10 more minutes.

4. Use immediately, or pour into an airtight container and store covered in the refrigerator until ready to use.

Cherry Barbecue Sauce

Yield: about 3 cups

Prep time: 10 minutes

Cook time: 30 minutes

1 cup ketchup

¼ cup dried cherries

1 cup water

⅓ cup tart cherry juice

¼ cup dark brown sugar

2 TB. molasses

1 TB. garlic powder

1 TB. black pepper

1 tsp. cayenne

1. In a small saucepan over medium heat, combine ketchup, dried cherries, water, tart cherry juice, dark brown sugar, molasses, garlic powder, black pepper, and cayenne, and stir constantly for 5 minutes.

2. Reduce heat to low, and simmer for 20 minutes, stirring occasionally.

3. Purée with a stick blender until smooth.

4. Use immediately, or pour into an airtight container and store covered in the refrigerator until ready to use.

CHEF'S TIP

You can brush Alabama Barbecue Sauce lightly over chicken, turkey, or pork during the last few minutes of grilling. This barbecue sauce is also great as a dipping sauce, so set some aside to serve at the table.

Brush Bourbon Glaze on foods at the end of their cooking process. With the higher sugar content, they will burn if it's added before cooking.

Chimichurri

Yield:
about 1 cup

Prep time:
10 minutes

1½ oz. (about 1 packed cup) fresh flat-leaf parsley

3 cloves garlic

2 tsp. dried oregano

2 TB. sherry vinegar

1 tsp. kosher salt

¼ tsp. red pepper flakes

½ cup olive oil

1. In a food processor, place flat-leaf parsley, garlic, oregano, sherry vinegar, kosher salt, and red pepper flakes, and pulse several times just to rough-chop the leaves.

2. In a small mixing bowl, add parsley mixture and olive oil, and whisk.

3. Use immediately, or pour into an airtight container and store covered in the refrigerator until ready to use.

Garlic-Herb Compound Butter

Yield:
1 pound (453.5 g)

Prep time:
20 minutes

1 lb. (453.5 g) unsalted butter, in chunks

1 tsp. garlic salt

2 cloves garlic, minced fine

⅛ tsp. fresh thyme leaves

⅛ tsp. fresh rosemary leaves, chopped

2 TB. lemon juice

1. In a food processor, place butter, garlic salt, garlic, thyme leaves, rosemary leaves, and lemon juice, and pulse until all ingredients are fully incorporated.

2. If not used immediately, pour butter into a small ice-cube tray, and freeze.

3. Use butter cubes as needed. Cubes can be kept for up to a year.

Kansas City Barbecue Sauce

Yield:
about 3 cups

Prep time:
10 minutes

Cook time:
30 minutes

1⅓ cups ketchup

1 cup water

⅓ cup apple cider vinegar

¼ cup dark brown sugar

2 TB. molasses

1 TB. onion powder

1 TB. garlic powder

1 TB. black pepper

1 tsp. celery salt

1 tsp. allspice

1 tsp. cayenne

1. In a small saucepan over medium heat, combine ketchup, water, apple cider vinegar, dark brown sugar, molasses, onion powder, garlic powder, black pepper, celery salt, allspice, and cayenne, and stir constantly for 5 minutes.

2. Reduce heat to low, and simmer for 20 minutes, stirring occasionally. Sauce should be thick.

3. Allow sauce to cool. Use immediately, or pour into an airtight container and store covered in the refrigerator until ready to use.

Memphis Barbecue Sauce

Yield: about 3 cups | **Prep time:** 15 minutes | **Cook time:** 25 minutes

2 TB. butter

¼ cup finely chopped yellow onion

2 TB. minced garlic

1 cup ketchup

½ cup water

2 TB. molasses

2 TB. prepared yellow mustard

2 TB. light brown sugar

1 TB. Worcestershire sauce

1 TB. paprika

1 TB. mild chili powder

2 tsp. dried oregano

2 tsp. dried thyme

1 tsp. kosher salt

1 tsp. black pepper

1 tsp. cayenne (optional)

1 cup apple cider vinegar

1. In a small saucepan over medium heat, melt butter.

2. Add yellow onion and garlic, and sauté until lightly browned.

3. Add ketchup, water, molasses, prepared yellow mustard, light brown sugar, Worcestershire sauce, paprika, mild chili powder, oregano, thyme, kosher salt, black pepper, cayenne (if using), and apple cider vinegar, and stir to combine. Make sure apple cider vinegar is added last.

4. Reduce heat, and simmer over low heat for 20 minutes.

5. Allow sauce to cool. Use immediately, or pour into an airtight container and store covered in the refrigerator until ready to use.

Peach Glaze

Yield: about 3 cups | **Prep time:** 10 minutes plus overnight rest time

1 cup peach preserves

1½ TB. Worcestershire sauce

1 TB. cracked black pepper

¼ tsp. ground ginger

1 fresh peach, peeled and minced

1. In a small mixing bowl, combine peach preserves, Worcestershire sauce, cracked black pepper, ginger, and peach.

2. Place plastic wrap over it, and allow to rest at room temperature overnight.

3. Mix again. Use immediately, or pour into an airtight container and store covered in the refrigerator until ready to use.

Pesto

Yield: about 1 cup | **Prep time:** 10 minutes

1½ oz. (about 2 packed cups) fresh basil leaves

3 cloves garlic

2 TB. pine nuts

1 tsp. kosher salt

⅓ cup grated Parmesan cheese

⅓ cup extra-virgin olive oil

1. In a food processor, place basil leaves, garlic, pine nuts, kosher salt, and Parmesan cheese, and pulse.

2. While the food processor is running, drizzle in extra-virgin olive oil.

3. Using a rubber spatula, scrape down the sides of the processor bowl, and pulse again until mixture is smooth.

4. Use immediately, or pour into an airtight container and store covered in the refrigerator until ready to use.

Sun-Dried Tomato Ketchup

Yield: about 2 cups

Prep time: 10 minutes

Cook time: 20 minutes

1 cup apple cider

½ cup oil-packed sun-dried tomatoes

¼ cup light brown sugar

¼ cup apple cider vinegar

¼ tsp. ground cloves

¼ tsp. ground ginger

¼ tsp. cayenne

½ yellow onion, diced

2 garlic cloves, minced

1 tsp. kosher salt

1. In a small saucepan over medium heat, combine apple cider, sun-dried tomatoes, light brown sugar, cider vinegar, cloves, ginger, cayenne, yellow onion, garlic, and kosher salt.

2. Simmer over medium heat for 15 minutes.

3. Purée with a stick blender until smooth.

4. Use immediately, or pour into an airtight container and store covered in the refrigerator until ready to use.

CHEF'S TIP

In recipes that call for puréeing the sauces with a stick blender, you can purée in a regular blender instead. But be sure to start on a low speed; if you start on a higher speed with hot liquids, they will burst out of the top of the lid.

Thai Sauce

Yield: about 1 cup

Prep time: 10 minutes

Cook time: 20 minutes

½ cup rice wine vinegar

⅓ cup light brown sugar

4 cloves garlic, minced

½ tsp. dried crushed chiles

1 TB. fish sauce

1 TB. soy sauce

1. In a small saucepan over medium heat, place rice wine vinegar, light brown sugar, garlic, chiles, fish sauce, and soy sauce, and bring to a simmer.

2. Simmer over medium heat for 15 minutes.

3. Use immediately, or pour into an airtight container and store covered in the refrigerator until ready to use.

Salsas

Salsa traditionally incorporates tomatoes, onions, and chiles with the cilantro herb. Other fruits can also be used with the tomatoes to produce different flavors. In the American Southwest, salsa is the main sauce and is served with most regional dishes.

Any of the salsas can be held in the refrigerator for 10 days, unless otherwise stated.

Corn Salsa

Yield:
1½ cups

Prep time:
15 minutes

1 cup (about 2 ears) uncooked corn kernels

2 plum tomatoes, seeded and diced

1 clove garlic, minced

1 jalapeño pepper, stemmed, seeded, and minced

1 TB. cilantro, chopped

2 TB. lime juice

1 tsp. kosher salt

1. In a medium mixing bowl, combine uncooked corn kernels, plum tomatoes, garlic, jalapeño pepper, cilantro, lime juice, and kosher salt.

2. Use immediately, or pour into an airtight container and store covered in the refrigerator until ready to use.

Papaya-Mint Salsa

Yield:
3 cups

Prep time:
15 minutes

1 papaya, peeled, seeded, and diced

4 ripe plum tomatoes, seeded and diced

1 red onion, diced

1 jalapeño pepper, stemmed, seeded, and minced

1 TB. cilantro, chopped

1 TB. mint, chopped

3 TB. lime juice

1. In a medium mixing bowl, combine papaya, plum tomatoes, red onion, jalapeño pepper, cilantro, mint, and lime juice.

2. Use immediately, or pour into an airtight container and store covered in the refrigerator until ready to use.

Salsa Verde

Yield:
1 pound (453.5 g)

Prep time:
15 minutes

12 tomatillos, husks removed and chopped rough

5 cloves garlic

1 white onion, chopped rough

3 TB. cilantro leaves, chopped

1 tsp. kosher salt

1 jalapeño pepper, stems and seeds removed

3 poblano peppers, stems and seeds removed and chopped rough

1 TB. lime juice

1. In a food processor, place tomatillos, garlic, white onion, cilantro leaves, kosher salt, jalapeño pepper, poblano peppers, and lime juice.

2. Pulse until all ingredients are incorporated; mixture should still be very chunky.

3. Use immediately, or pour into an airtight container and store covered in the refrigerator until ready to use.

Watermelon-Jicama Salsa

Yield:
3 cups

Prep time:
15 minutes

2 cups watermelon, diced small

1 cup jicama, diced small

1 jalapeño pepper, minced fine

1 TB. cilantro, chopped

1 TB. mint, chopped

3 TB. lime juice

1. In a medium mixing bowl, combine watermelon, jicama, jalapeño pepper, cilantro, mint, and lime juice.

2. Use immediately, or pour into an airtight container and store covered in the refrigerator until ready to use.

WHAT IS JICAMA?

Jicama is a tuber that has a mild, almost citrus flavor. It provides a nice, crunchy texture to whatever it's added to.

Rubs

Rubs are a collection of spices used with different grilled foods. A large portion of the rubs are salts and sugars. Because of the salt and sugar chemical properties, they add a preservative quality to what they are rubbed into.

Rubs are shelf stable and can be kept for a year without a loss in quality.

Cajun Rub

Yield:
2 cups

Prep time:
10 minutes

½ cup paprika

6 TB. kosher salt

¼ cup black pepper, coarsely ground

2 TB. ground white pepper

3 TB. garlic powder

2 TB. onion powder

3 TB. dried oregano

2 TB. dried thyme

2 TB. cayenne

1. In a small mixing bowl, combine paprika, kosher salt, black pepper, white pepper, garlic powder, onion powder, oregano, thyme, and cayenne.

2. Use immediately, or pour into an airtight container and store covered in the pantry until ready to use.

Chipotle Rub

Yield:
1 cup

Prep time:
10 minutes

3 dried chipotle peppers

3 TB. black pepper

¼ cup light brown sugar

¼ cup kosher salt

1 TB. dried Mexican oregano

1 TB. dried cilantro leaves

1 tsp. cumin

1 tsp. onion powder

1 tsp. dry orange peel

1. In a small mixing bowl, combine chipotle peppers, black pepper, light brown sugar, kosher salt, Mexican oregano, cilantro leaves, cumin, onion powder, and dry orange peel.

2. Use immediately, or pour into an airtight container and store covered in the pantry until ready to use.

Curry Rub

Yield:
2 cups

Prep time:
10 minutes

½ cup ground curry powder

¼ cup ground turmeric

¼ cup ground paprika

¼ cup ground ginger

½ cup kosher salt

¼ cup light brown sugar

1. In a medium mixing bowl, combine curry powder, turmeric, paprika, ginger, kosher salt, and light brown sugar.

2. Use immediately, or pour into an airtight container and store covered in the pantry until ready to use.

Garlic-Tarragon Rub

Yield:
2 cups

Prep time:
10 minutes

1 TB. onion powder

5 cloves garlic, minced

2 TB. parsley, chopped

1 TB. thyme leaves

6 TB. tarragon leaves, chopped

2 TB. lemon zest

1 TB. lime zest

3 TB. kosher salt

1. In a small mixing bowl, combine onion powder, garlic, parsley, thyme leaves, tarragon leaves, lemon zest, lime zest, and kosher salt.

2. Use immediately, or pour into an airtight container and store covered in the refrigerator until ready to use.

Lemon-Coriander Rub

Yield:
1 cup

Prep time:
10 minutes

2 TB. smoked paprika

3 TB. lemon zest

3 TB. crushed coriander

3 TB. light brown sugar

4 TB. kosher salt

1 TB. white pepper

1. In a small mixing bowl, combine smoked paprika, lemon zest, coriander, light brown sugar, kosher salt, and white pepper.

2. Use immediately, or pour into an airtight container and store covered in the pantry until ready to use.

Jamaican Jerk Rub

Yield:
2½ cups

Prep time:
10 minutes

½ cup malt vinegar

¼ cup white rum

2 habanero peppers, stemmed, seeded, and minced

1 red onion, chopped

¼ cup vegetable oil

¼ cup kosher salt

2 TB. ground black pepper

¼ cup ground allspice

1 TB. ground cinnamon

1 tsp. ground nutmeg

1 TB. ground ginger

1 TB. molasses

1. In a food processor, place malt vinegar, white rum, habanero peppers, red onion, vegetable oil, kosher salt, black pepper, allspice, cinnamon, nutmeg, ginger, and molasses.

2. Pulse ingredients until smooth.

3. Use immediately, or pour into an airtight container and store covered in the refrigerator until ready to use.

HOT PEPPER WARNING

When working with hot chile peppers, wear gloves to keep the spicy capsicum oils off your hands. If you get the oils on your hands, they can be difficult to remove. That means if you don't wear gloves and then touch your eyes, you'll regret it.

Mediterranean Rub

Yield:
1 cup

Prep time:
10 minutes

4 TB. fresh thyme leaves

4 TB. fresh oregano leaves, chopped

2 TB. fresh rosemary leaves, chopped

1 TB. lemon zest

2 cloves garlic, minced fine

cup kosher salt

1. In a small mixing bowl, combine thyme leaves, oregano leaves, rosemary leaves, lemon zest, garlic, and kosher salt.

2. Use immediately, or pour into an airtight container and store covered in the refrigerator until ready to use.

Memphis Barbecue Rub

Yield:
1 cup

¼ cup paprika

¼ cup dark brown sugar

2 TB. black pepper

1 TB. kosher salt

Prep time:
10 minutes

1 tsp. celery salt

2 tsp. garlic powder

2 tsp. dry mustard

2 tsp. cumin

1 tsp. cayenne

1. In a small mixing bowl, combine paprika, dark brown sugar, black pepper, kosher salt, celery salt, garlic powder, dry mustard, cumin, and cayenne.

2. Use immediately, or pour into an airtight container and store covered in the pantry until ready to use.

Texas Brisket Rub

Yield:
1 cup

2 TB. black pepper

1 TB. cayenne

¼ cup chili powder

¼ cup kosher salt

Prep time:
10 minutes

¼ cup dark brown sugar

2 tsp. garlic powder

2 tsp. dry mustard

2 tsp. cumin

1. In a small mixing bowl, combine black pepper, cayenne, chili powder, kosher salt, dark brown sugar, garlic powder, dry mustard, and cumin.

2. Use immediately, or pour into an airtight container and store covered in the pantry until ready to use.

CHEF'S TIP

Most dry spices and herbs will lose flavor over time. When purchasing the dry ingredients, look for containers that have a date on them, or buy directly from a spice manufacturer. When they're 1 year old, discard and buy fresh replacements.

Marinades

Marinades by definition are used to give the meat flavor and help tenderize it before cooking. These marinades can be held in the refrigerator for 10 days, unless otherwise stated.

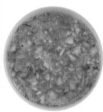

Allium Marinade

Yield:
1½ cups

Prep time:
10 minutes

¼ cup lemon juice

¼ cup sauvignon blanc wine

¼ cup olive oil

2 TB. thyme leaves

4 shallots, minced

2 TB. kosher salt

1. In a small mixing bowl, combine lemon juice, sauvignon blanc wine, olive oil, thyme leaves, shallots, and kosher salt.

2. Use immediately, or pour into an airtight container and store covered in the refrigerator until ready to use.

Asian Marinade

Yield:
2 cups

Prep time:
10 minutes

½ cup soy sauce

¼ cup fish sauce

¾ cup rice wine vinegar

¼ cup honey

¼ cup sesame oil

6 cloves garlic, minced

1 TB. ginger, grated

1 TB. green onion, chopped

2 TB. sesame seeds

2 TB. white pepper

1. In a small mixing bowl, combine soy sauce, fish sauce, rice wine vinegar, honey, sesame oil, garlic, ginger, green onion, sesame seeds, and white pepper.

2. Use immediately, or pour into an airtight container and store covered in the refrigerator until ready to use.

Athenian Marinade

Yield:
2 cups

Prep time:
10 minutes

½ cup plain Greek yogurt

5 cloves garlic, minced

1 TB. lemon juice

3 TB. vegetable oil

1 TB. honey

1 tsp. chili powder

1 TB. ground ginger

2 TB. kosher salt

1 tsp. ground cumin

1. In a small mixing bowl, combine plain Greek yogurt, garlic, lemon juice, vegetable oil, honey, chili powder, ginger, kosher salt, and cumin.

2. Use immediately, or pour into an airtight container and store covered in the refrigerator until ready to use.

Citrus-Fennel Marinade

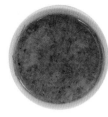

Yield:
2 cups

Prep time:
10 minutes

¼ cup orange juice

1 TB. lemon zest

2 TB. lime juice

1 tsp. lime zest

¼ cup fennel tops,
chopped

1 TB. fennel seeds

2 TB. kosher salt

¼ cup honey

¼ cup vegetable oil

4 cloves garlic, minced

1 TB. ground cumin

1. In a small mixing bowl, combine orange juice, lemon zest, lime juice, lime zest, fennel tops, fennel seeds, kosher salt, honey, vegetable oil, garlic, and cumin.

2. Use immediately, or pour into an airtight container and store covered in the refrigerator until ready to use.

Coconut Marinade

Yield:
2 cups

Prep time:
10 minutes

6 TB. lime juice

½ cup cream of coconut, such as Coco Lopez

¼ cup white rum

2 TB. green onions,
chopped

3 TB. cilantro leaves,
chopped

2 jalapeño peppers,
stemmed, seeded,
and minced

1 TB. kosher salt

1 tsp. white pepper

1. In a small mixing bowl, combine lime juice, cream of coconut, white rum, green onions, cilantro leaves, jalapeño peppers, kosher salt, and white pepper.

2. Use immediately, or pour into an airtight container and store covered in the refrigerator until ready to use.

Orange-Ale Marinade

Yield:
2½ cups

Prep time:
10 minutes

2 TB. cilantro leaves,
chopped

1 clove garlic, minced

1 TB. orange zest

1 cup orange juice

1 cup summer-style ale

2 TB. soy sauce

1 TB. toasted sesame
oil

2 TB. kosher salt

1. In a small mixing bowl, combine cilantro leaves, garlic, orange zest, orange juice, summer-style ale, soy sauce, toasted sesame oil, and kosher salt.

2. Use immediately, or pour into an airtight container and store covered in the refrigerator until ready to use.

BEEF

GRILL METHOD:
DIRECT HEAT

PREP TIME:
5 MIN.

COOK TIME:
10-20 MIN.

SERVES: 4

Basic Grilled Steaks

When I think of grilling out, the first thing I think of is a big, juicy steak. But too often, I go to a cookout and get a big, dry steak. If you follow this recipe, you'll have people asking for your grilling secrets. Time after time, the items with the least number of ingredients and steps are the foods people like the most.

INGREDIENTS

4 (less than 1 ½-in. [3.75-cm] thick) New York strip, T-bone, filet mignon, or porterhouse steaks

2 TB. kosher salt

¼ TB. black pepper

¼ cup vegetable oil

TOOLS

Transport tray

Paper towel

Tongs

Squirt bottle filled with water

Meat thermometer

Serving platter

PREP

Medium

Preheat the grill to medium for direct-heat cooking.

Lay steaks out on a transport tray, and blot dry with a paper towel to aid in the browning process.

Season both sides of steaks with kosher salt and black pepper.

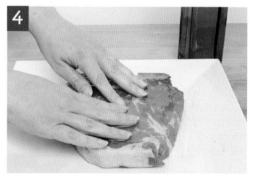

Rub down steaks with vegetable oil, evenly dispersing it, to help conduct the heat from the grill to them.

CHEF'S TIP

If you sprinkle the seasonings from several inches above the meat, it will spread more evenly. This will help to eliminate the problem of food tasting salty in one bite and bland in the next.

GRILL

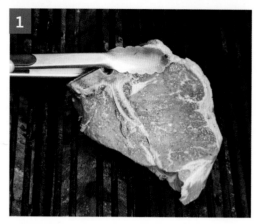

Using tongs, place steaks on the hottest part of the grill over direct heat, and allow to cook for 2 minutes. If flames start to burn up from the bottom of the grill, give them a squirt of water with the squirt bottle.

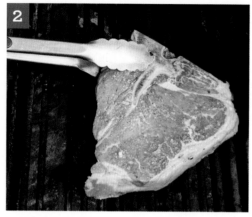

Rotate steaks 45 degrees to make the cross-hatch pattern, and cook for 2 minutes. If steaks stick to the grill as you're trying to do this, just wait another minute and then rotate.

Flip over steaks, and repeat the process on the other side.

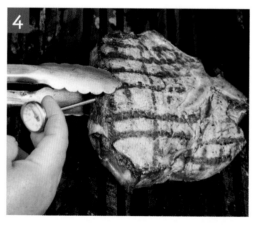

Put a meat thermometer in steak to check doneness (see the "How Do You Like Your Steak?" table), making sure at least 1 full inch (2.5 cm) of the thermometer stem is in meat.

5

When the desired temperature is reached, remove steaks from the grill and place on a serving platter. Allow steaks to rest for 5 minutes to allow juices to redistribute evenly. Serve.

HOW DO YOU LIKE YOUR STEAK?

Doneness	Internal Temperature	How It Looks
Rare	125°F (52°C)	Lightly charred on the outside, browned around the sides, and bright red in the middle
Medium-rare	135°F (57°C)	Well-browned sides, with the top and bottom charred to a dark brown color; the center is mostly pink with a little red
Medium	145°F (63°C)	A rich brown color on the sides, with the top and bottom charred darkly (but not black); the middle has a thick band of light pink that's more browned than pink
Medium-well	155°F (68°C)	A dark-brown surface with good charring on the top and bottom and a hint of pink in the middle
Well	165°F (74°C)	A dark-brown surface (not burnt) with a middle that's browned through

GRILL METHOD:
DIRECT HEAT

PREP TIME:
5 MIN.

COOK TIME:
10-20 MIN.

SERVES: 4

T-Bone
with Bourbon Glaze

Once you know have the idea of how to do a basic steak, it's easy to spice things up. In this case, I'm using a T-bone steak, but you could use any type of steak with this recipe. The T-bone is one of my favorites because you get a little tenderloin steak and New York strip steak together, only separated by the bone. When meat is bone-in, it will tend to be juicier and much more flavorful. (And if you have a dog, it'll be happy at the end of the night to gnaw on it.) Finishing with a Bourbon glaze adds a hint of sweetness and complexity that takes the flavor of the steak to the next level.

INGREDIENTS

4 T-bone steaks

2 TB. kosher salt

¼ TB. black pepper

¼ cup vegetable oil

1 cup Bourbon Glaze (see "Seasonings and Condiments")

TOOLS

Transport tray

Paper towel

Tongs

Squirt bottle filled with water

Meat thermometer

Sauce brush

Serving platter

PREP

Preheat the grill to medium for direct-heat cooking.

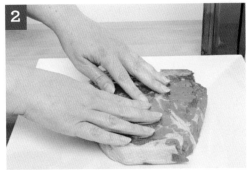

Place T-bones on a transport tray, and dry with a paper towel. Season with kosher salt and black pepper, and rub down evenly with vegetable oil.

GRILL

Using tongs, place T-bones on the hottest part of the grill over direct heat, and turn every 1 minute to form the cross-hatch pattern on each side. Remember, if they stick to the grill as you're trying to do this, just wait another minute. If flames leap up, squirt them with water using the squirt bottle.

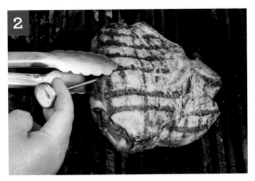

Put a meat thermometer in T-bone to check doneness, making sure at least 1 full inch (2.5 cm) of the thermometer stem is in meat. Don't let the probe get too close to the bone; this will give you a hot reading.

When you're 10° from reaching the desired temperature, move T-bones to the coolest area of the grill. Brush both sides of T-bones with Bourbon Glaze using a sauce brush, cover the grill, and cook for 5 minutes.

Remove T-bones from the grill, place on a serving platter, and allow to rest for 5 minutes. Serve; the steaks will have a gorgeous glow that accents the grill marks.

GRILL METHOD:
DIRECT HEAT

PREP TIME:
25 MIN.

COOK TIME:
10-20 MIN.

SERVES: 4

Rib-Eye
with Garlic-Tarragon Rub

This version of the basic grilled steak has a rub applied before cooking to enhance the rich, complex flavors. The rib-eye is a steak-lover's steak that comes from a little-used muscle—the upper rib section, a part that doesn't hold any of the steer's weight. The rib-eye has bountiful amounts of intramuscular marbling to keep it tender, which adds to the beefy flavor that comes out when grilled.

INGREDIENTS

4 (6- to 8-oz. [170- to 226.75-g])
   rib-eye steaks

2 TB. yellow mustard

¼ cup Garlic-Tarragon Rub
   (see "Seasonings and Condiments")

Pan spray

TOOLS

Transport tray

Paper towel

Tongs

Squirt bottle filled with water

Meat thermometer

Serving platter

PREP

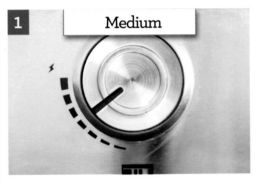

Preheat the grill to medium for direct-heat cooking.

Place rib-eyes on a transport tray, and dry with a paper towel. Rub a thin layer of yellow mustard over surface of steaks.

Coat rib-eyes on all sides with Garlic-Tarragon Rub, making sure there's a good coating all the way around steaks, and allow to rest for 20 minutes.

Put a thin layer of pan spray on top of rub. Most spices are oil-soluble, so putting a layer of pan spray on top of rub allows spices to melt into oil and season steaks.

GRILL

Using tongs, place rib-eyes on the hottest part of the grill over direct heat, and turn every 1 minute to form the cross-hatch pattern on each side. If flames start to burn up from the bottom of the grill, give them a squirt of water with the squirt bottle.

Put a thermometer in rib-eye to check doneness, making sure that at least 1 full inch (2.5 cm) of the thermometer stem is in meat. Remove from the grill when you are 5° from reaching the desired temperature, and allow to rest on a serving platter for 5 minutes. Serve.

GRILL METHOD:
DIRECT HEAT

PREP TIME:
5 MIN.

COOK TIME:
10-20 MIN.

SERVES: 4

BEEF

Strip Steaks
with Chimichurri

The strip steak, or New York strip, is the larger section of a T-bone. This cut is tender but still has a little bite, making it the Goldilocks of steaks: just right. Great flavor and marbling also make this a perfect choice for grilling. In this recipe, I am doing an Argentine variation and serving it with a chimichurri sauce. This sauce brings some heat and a lot of acid to the game, washing away the oils with each bite and leaving you wanting more.

INGREDIENTS

4 strip steaks

2 TB. kosher salt

1 tsp. black pepper

¼ cup vegetable oil

2 cups Chimichurri (see "Seasonings and Condiments")

TOOLS

Transport tray

Paper towel

Tongs

Squirt bottle filled with water

Sauce ramekins

Meat thermometer

Serving platter

PREP

Preheat the grill to medium for direct-heat cooking.

Lay strip steaks on a transport tray, and blot dry with a paper towel. Season on both sides with kosher salt and black pepper, and rub down evenly with vegetable oil.

GRILL

Using tongs, place strip steaks on the hottest part of the grill over direct heat, and turn every 2 minutes to form the cross-hatch pattern on both sides. If flames come up from the bottom of the grill, give them a squirt of water with the squirt bottle.

Put a meat thermometer in strip steak to check doneness. Remove each steak from the grill when about 5° short of where you want them to be; carryover cooking will take it the rest of the way. Place on a serving platter, and allow to rest for 5 minutes so steak has time to relax and become tender again.

Pour ¼ cup Chimichurri Sauce into 4 sauce ramekins, and serve on the side of strip steaks for dipping.

GRILL METHOD:
DIRECT HEAT

PREP TIME:
5 MIN.

COOK TIME:
10-20 MIN.

SERVES: 4

Filet Mignon
with Cherry Barbecue Sauce

Filet mignon is a steak cut from the tenderloin and is the most tender cut of beef. It doesn't have much marbling, which is good if you're trying to watch your weight; however, this makes it a little harder to cook correctly. Fat in the marbling helps to transport heat into the middle of the meat, so when cooking a filet mignon, you need to slow down the heat a bit. In this recipe, I have paired the steak with a cherry barbecue sauce. Cherries bring out a robust floral component in beef, especially grass-finished beef.

INGREDIENTS

4 (6- to 8-oz. [170- to 226.75-g])
   filet mignon steaks

2 TB. kosher salt

¼ TB. black pepper

¼ cup vegetable oil

1 cup Cherry Barbecue Sauce
   (see "Seasonings and Condiments")

TOOLS

Transport tray

Paper towel

Tongs

Squirt bottle filled with water

Meat thermometer

Sauce brush

Serving platter

PREP

Medium-Low

Preheat the grill to medium-low for direct-heat cooking.

Place filet mignon on a transport tray, and dry with a paper towel. Season with kosher salt and black pepper, and rub down evenly with vegetable oil.

GRILL

Using tongs, place filet mignon on the grill over direct heat, and turn every 2 minutes to form the cross-hatch pattern on each side. When flames start leaping up from the grill, squirt the base of the flame with the squirt bottle.

Put a meat thermometer in filet mignon to check doneness, making sure at least 1 full inch (2.5 cm) of the thermometer stem is in meat.

When you're 10° from reaching the desired temperature, brush top of filet mignon with Cherry Barbecue Sauce using a sauce brush, cover the grill, and cook for 5 minutes.

Remove filet mignon from the grill, and put on a serving platter. Pour any remaining Cherry Barbecue Sauce over filet mignon, and allow to rest for 5 minutes. Serve.

GRILL METHOD:
DIRECT HEAT

PREP TIME:
5 MIN.

COOK TIME:
10-20 MIN.

SERVES: 4

BEEF

Porterhouse
with Garlic-Herb Compound Butter

The porterhouse cut could be referred to as a T-bone steak all grown up—the tenderloin portion of the T-bone must be a minimum width of ½ inch (1.25 cm), while the porterhouse is required to be 1¼ inches (3.25 cm) wide. This means the sirloin portion of the porterhouse is also substantially larger, making it something that could be shared among a couple of friends. The Italians serve porterhouse steaks blood rare with salt, pepper, and herbs, which is similar to what I'm doing in this recipe. However, feel free to cook them longer if that's your preference.

INGREDIENTS

2 porterhouse steaks

2 TB. kosher salt

1 tsp. black pepper

¼ cup vegetable oil

½ cup Garlic-Herb Compound Butter
  (see "Seasonings and Condiments")

TOOLS

Transport tray

Paper towel

Tongs

Cutting board

Sharp chef's knife

Squirt bottle filled with water

Meat thermometer

Serving platter

PREP

1 Medium

Preheat the grill to medium for direct-heat cooking.

2

Lay porterhouse steaks out on a transport tray, and blot dry with a paper towel. Season both sides with kosher salt and black pepper, and rub down evenly with vegetable oil.

GRILL

1

Using tongs, place porterhouse steaks on the hottest part of the grill over direct heat, and turn every 2 minutes to form the cross-hatch pattern on both sides. If flames come up from the bottom of the grill, give them a squirt of water with the squirt bottle.

2

Put a meat thermometer in porterhouse steak to check doneness. Remove from the grill when steaks are about 5° short of where you want them to be; carryover cooking will take it the rest of the way.

3

Remove steaks from the grill, put on a cutting board, and allow to rest for 5 minutes. Using a sharp chef's knife, remove bone from each, and slice into strips. Arrange strips on a serving platter, top with slices of Garlic-Herb Compound Butter, and serve.

GRILL METHOD:
DIRECT HEAT

PREP TIME:
24 HR.

COOK TIME:
12 MIN.

SERVES: 4

BEEF

Hamburgers

Grilling a hamburger evokes special memories of warm summer days on the patio with family and friends hovering near the grill discussing the latest events over a cool beverage. When making a burger, the goal is a finished product that's juicy and layered with complexity. Achieving this goal involves properly selecting and grinding the meat, not overworking it, and maintaining constant grill temperature. If you have a grinder attachment for your mixer, use it to prepare your burger blend. If not, purchase 80 percent lean ground meat.

INGREDIENTS

1 lb. (453.5 g) beef short rib meat, cut into 1-in. (2.5-cm) pieces

2 lb. (907 g) beef sirloin, cut into 1-in. (2.5-cm) pieces

Or

3 lb. (1.5 kg) ground sirloin, 80/20

4 hamburger buns

1 TB. kosher salt

Pan spray

Vegetables and condiments of your choice

TOOLS

Mixing bowl

Meat grinder *or* stand mixer with grinder attachments

Plastic wrap

Sharp chef's knife

Cutting board

Transport tray

Squirt bottle filled with water

Offset spatula

Meat thermometer

Serving platter

GRIND

If you have 3 pounds ground sirloin, skip to Prep 5.

In a large mixing bowl, combine beef short rib meat, beef sirloin, and kosher salt. Place bowl in the refrigerator, and allow to rest, uncovered, for 24 hours.

Place the grinder attachments in the freezer overnight so meat doesn't get above 38°F (3°C) during the grinding process; otherwise, it'll be dry.

Bring out hamburger meat and grinder attachments. Assemble the grinder to the manufacturer's specifications for a medium grind, and begin grinding. As meat comes through the grinder, feed the resulting long strands onto plastic wrap.

Layer hamburger meat strands on top of one another until you have a 6-inch (15.25-cm) diameter roll of ground meat.

PREP

If you purchased your meat already ground, start here

For purchased ground sirloin, transfer to a long piece of plastic wrap. For both preground and just-ground hamburger meat, roll the plastic wrap around meat, creating a long tube of meat 6 inches (15.25 cm) thick.

Cut tube every 1 inch (2.5 cm) for individual hamburger patties, and place on a transport tray. Reshape hamburger patties as needed to maintain shape.

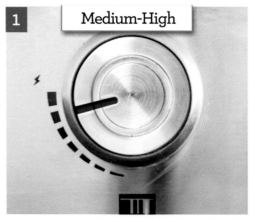

Preheat the grill to medium-high for direct-heat cooking. Spray top and bottom of hamburgers with pan spray.

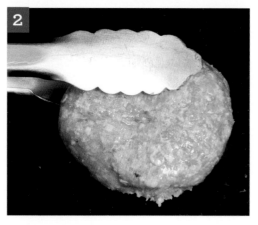

Using tongs, place hamburgers on the grill over direct heat, and cook for 2 minutes. If flames flare up from the coals, spray a small amount of water on them with the squirt bottle.

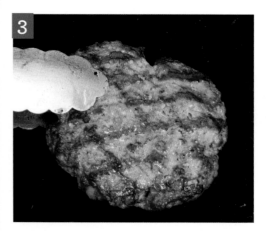

Rotate hamburgers 45 degrees to produce the cross-hatch pattern, and allow to cook for 2 minutes. Flip hamburgers, and repeat the process on the other side.

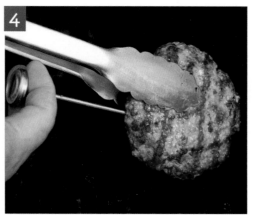

Check doneness of each hamburger using a meat thermometer. If they haven't reached 165°F (74°C; see "How Do You Like Your Steak?" table for variations), move them to a cooler part of the grill, cover, and check every 10 minutes until the correct temperature is achieved.

5

Remove hamburgers from the grill. Place hamburger buns on a serving platter, place hamburgers on top, and serve vegetables and condiments of your choice.

CHEF'S TIP

Cooking with the grill lid open will result in a better crust on the outside of the meat.

ADDING FLARE TO YOUR HAMBURGER

You can add regional flavor to the hamburger by grinding or mixing in different ingredients. The styles in the following table will give your burgers a true zing.

Style	Ingredients
All-American	1 TB. dried onions 1 TB. Worcestershire sauce
English	1 tsp. curry powder 3 TB. raisins
Napa	3 TB. dry red wine 2 TB. minced sun-dried tomatoes
Southwest	3 TB. roasted corn 1 TB. minced green chile peppers (Anaheim or jalapeño)
Texas	1 TB. brisket rub 4 TB. cooked brisket, chopped
Thai	1 tsp. hot chile peppers, minced 1 tsp. garlic, minced 1 tsp. ginger, minced 1 TB. green onion, minced 1 TB. cilantro, chopped

GRILL METHOD:
INDIRECT HEAT

PREP TIME:
20 MIN.

COOK TIME:
1 HR.

SERVES: 12

Beef Tenderloin

Beef tenderloin is the most delicate cut of beef, with a fine grain that makes it tender without a lot of fat. Most people know of the tenderloin as a filet mignon, which is what it's called when it's cut into steaks. This recipe uses indirect heat to roast the entire tenderloin at one time. Then, once it's cooked, the beef tenderloin is sliced into individual slices.

INGREDIENTS

1 (about 4-lb. [1.75-kg]) whole beef tenderloin, peeled and with side muscle on

3 TB. kosher salt

1 TB. black pepper

¼ cup vegetable oil

TOOLS

Cutting boards

Sharp boning knife

Butcher's twine

Disposable aluminum roasting pan

Tongs

Squirt bottle filled with water

In-oven meat thermometer

Sharp slicing knife

Serving platter

PREP

1 On a cutting board, pull off most of tenderloin fat and thin membrane under fat by hand.

2 Using a sharp boning knife, cut under thin membrane of tenderloin while pulling back on it with your other hand at the same time. You should be able to cut off strips of silverskin (gristle) without cutting into meat.

3 Fold under last little bit of pointy end (tail) of tenderloin to give you a more consistent width.

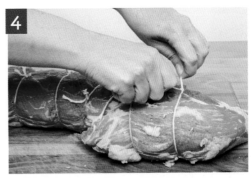

4 Using butcher's twine, tie tenderloin every 2 inches (5 cm) so entire length is about the same width for even cooking.

5 Liberally season tenderloin on all sides with kosher salt and black pepper, and rub down with vegetable oil.

CHEF'S TIP

When served with French rolls, beef tenderloin makes great gourmet sliders.

GRILL

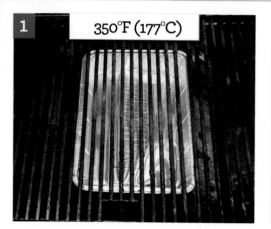

1 350°F (177°C)

Preheat the grill to 350°F (177°C) for indirect-heat cooking. Put a disposable aluminum roasting pan under the grate to catch dripping juices.

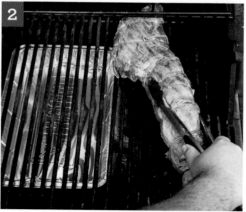

2

Using tongs, place tenderloin on the grill over direct heat, and turn every 2 minutes to sear on all sides. If flames start to burn up from the bottom of the grill, give them a squirt of water with the squirt bottle.

3

Move tenderloin over roasting pan, and place an in-oven meat thermometer in thickest part of meat.

4 1 hour

Cover the grill, and cook for 1 hour, maintaining a temperature of 350°F (177°C) and not opening the grill again until your thermometer says 135°F (57°C).

Remove tenderloin from the grill, put on a clean cutting board, and allow to rest for 15 minutes to allow juices to spread out again.

Tenderloin should now be a perfect medium-rare. Slice to your desired thickness across the grain using a sharp slicing knife, place on a serving platter, and serve.

EFFECTS OF OPENING A GRILL WHEN INDIRECT-HEAT COOKING

When you're indirect-heat cooking, you're essentially baking. This means it's important to have a steady heat in the grill to make food appropriately. Most grills don't have a heavy insulated exterior to maintain temperature. Knowing that heat rises, when you open the lid of the grill, all the heat takes off like a helium balloon. When you close the lid again, the grill has to start all over again to heat the air inside. This means the food will take longer to cook, drying out the exterior of the product.

Moisture also plays a role in the cooking process. With most things that are roasted, the moisture from the food hovers around the outside of it. Upon opening the lid of a grill, the moisture is quick to evaporate in the temperature change. So when you close the lid again, more moisture is sucked out of the food. This could create a dried-out piece of food.

GRILL METHOD:
INDIRECT HEAT

PREP TIME:
20 MIN. + 24 HR.

COOK TIME:
2 HR.

SERVES: 12

Prime Rib

I think of prime rib as a special weekend treat, because most restaurants in my area have it on their menus only on Friday and Saturday. This roast comes from the top of the ribcage area and is a very tender cut of meat with great marbling. Because of this, when prime rib is slow roasted, it melts away in your mouth, leaving the salty, rich flavor of the cooked meat. Cooking it on the grill adds a smoky character that can't be attained in the household oven.

INGREDIENTS

3 TB. kosher salt

1 TB. black pepper

1 TB. garlic salt

1 tsp. dried thyme

1 tsp. fresh rosemary, minced

½ tsp. celery salt

1 (6-lb. [2.75-kg]) beef rib roast or 6-rib standing rib roast

½ cup wood chips

2 cups beef stock (optional)

TOOLS

Mixing bowl

Paper towels

Cooling rack

Sheet pan

Disposable aluminum roasting pan

Tongs

In-oven meat thermometer

Aluminum foil

Rimless cookie sheet

Cutting board

Sharp slicing knife

Serving platter

Meat fork

PREP

In a small mixing bowl, combine kosher salt, black pepper, garlic salt, thyme, rosemary, and celery salt.

Dry prime rib with paper towels, and rub seasoning mix into all parts.

Put a cooling rack on top of a sheet pan, and place prime rib fat side down on the cooling rack.

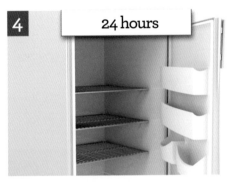

24 hours

Place in the refrigerator, and allow to rest for 24 hours. This allows exterior of prime rib to dry out, which will let some of the smoke flavor penetrate meat during grilling.

GRILLING TRIVIA

Many people may know prime rib as a standing rib roast. The name changed over time when butchering processes became more automated and the prices of meat began to come down. During that time, prime rib started to be consumed by more people. In parts of England, it became known as "Sunday Roast." It would often be served with Yorkshire pudding, vegetables, and gravy.

GRILL

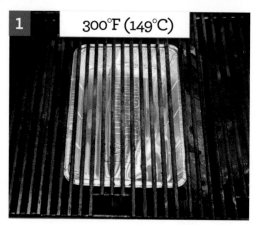

1 300°F (149°C)

Preheat the grill to 300°F (149°C) for indirect-heat cooking. Put a disposable aluminum roasting pan under the grate to catch dripping juices.

2

Using tongs, place prime rib fat side down on the grate over the drip pan, and place an in-oven meat thermometer in thickest part of meat.

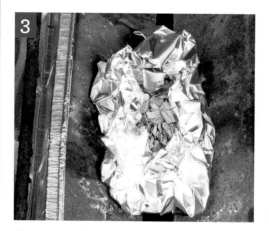

3

On a square of aluminum foil, place wood chips and roll up, leaving one end open. Put wrapped wood chips on the hot part of the grill bed.

4 2 hours

Cover the grill, and cook for 2 hours, maintaining a temperature of 300°F (149°C) and not opening the grill until the thermometer says prime rib has reached 125°F (52°C).

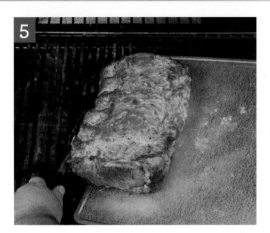

Slide prime rib onto a rimless cookie sheet to remove from the grill, place on a clean cutting board, and allow to rest for 15 minutes.

Remove the roasting pan from the grill. Strain, degrease, and taste accumulated drippings or au jus, adjusting taste by adding kosher salt, black pepper, and beef stock as needed.

Prime rib should now be a perfect medium-rare. On a cutting board, slice to your desired thickness across the grain using a sharp slicing knife, and place on a serving platter with a meat fork for pickup. Serve with au jus.

GRILL METHOD:
SMOKING

PREP TIME:
20 MIN. + 24 HR.

COOK TIME:
14 HR.

SERVES: 10

Brisket
with Kansas City Barbecue Sauce

A good brisket has a crisp, flavorful bark on the outside with a mahogany smoke ring that penetrates into the meat. The sweet, salty tang of the spices used in this recipe complements the brisket and helps wake up your taste buds. Because the animal carries 60 percent of its weight on this muscle, it's a tough cut of meat, meaning you have to cook it slow and let the natural moisture in the product break down that connective tissue. There's very little fat in this to begin with, so you need to take care to purchase USDA Choice or Prime certified (or an EU fat rating of 4 or 5). And make sure both muscles are still attached (the point and the flat).

INGREDIENTS

1 (10- to 12-lb. [4.5- to 5.5-kg]) beef brisket, deckle off and boneless

½ cup yellow mustard

1 cup Texas Brisket Rub (see "Seasonings and Condiments")

2 cups wood chips

20 slices white bread

Kansas City Barbecue Sauce (see "Seasonings and Condiments")

TOOLS

Cutting boards

Paper towels

Sharp chef's knife

Cooling rack

Sheet pan

Disposable aluminum roasting pan

Tongs

In-oven meat thermometer

Aluminum foil

Rimless cookie sheet

Sharp slicing knife

Serving platter

Meat fork

PREP

On a cutting board, dry brisket with paper towels. Using a sharp chef's knife, cut any exterior fat down to about ¼ inch (.5 cm) thick.

Rub yellow mustard, followed by ½ cup Texas Brisket Rub, into all parts of brisket.

Put a cooling rack on top of a sheet pan, and put the brisket fat side down onto the cooling rack. Put in the refrigerator, and allow to rest for 24 hours to let exterior of meat to dry out, which enables the smoke flavor to penetrate it.

Rub remaining ½ cup Texas Brisket Rub into the brisket.

WHAT IS A DECKLE?

Deckle refers to the fatty layer on top of the meat.

GRILL

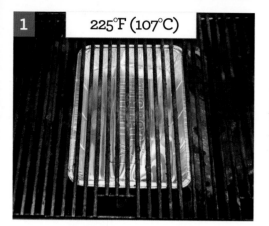

1 225°F (107°C)

Preheat the grill to 225°F (107°C) for smoking. Put a disposable aluminum roasting pan under the grate to catch dripping juices.

2

Using tongs, place brisket fat side down on the grate over the roasting pan for indirect cooking. Place an in-oven probe thermometer in thickest part of meat, making sure it isn't in fat between two muscles.

3

On a square of aluminum foil, place wood chips and roll up, leaving one end open. Place wrapped wood chips on the hot bed of the grill.

4 14 hours

Immediately cover the grill, and smoke for 14 hours, maintaining a temperature of 225°F (107°C) and not opening the grill again until the thermometer says brisket has reached 192°F (89°C).

5

Slide brisket onto a rimless cookie sheet to remove from the grill, place on a clean cutting board, and allow to rest for 15 minutes.

6

Separate flat from point using a sharp slicing knife. Cut point into 1-inch (2.5-cm) cubes.

7

Return point to the grill to finish your "burnt ends."

8

Slice flat across the grain at ¼-inch (.5-cm) thickness, and shingle onto a serving platter. Serve with white bread slices and Kansas City Barbecue Sauce to taste on the side.

GRILL METHOD:
SMOKING

PREP TIME:
20 MIN.

COOK TIME:
6 HR.

SERVES: 4

Short Ribs
with Chipotle Rub

Most people think of pork ribs when grilling or barbecuing; however, the flavor of beef marries well with spicy and smoky flavors. Beef short ribs have more meat on the bone, and by combining a chipotle rub with these ribs, you develop that intense combination of spice and smoke. It may be hard to find these at just any store; you may need to go to the major chain or warehouse stores.

INGREDIENTS

2 boneless beef short rib sections

½ cup yellow mustard

1 cup Chipotle Rub (see "Seasonings and Condiments")

2 cups wood chips

TOOLS

Disposable aluminum roasting pan

Cutting boards

Paper towels

Sharp chef's knives

Carrying tray

Aluminum foil

Tongs

Serving platter

PREP

225°F (107°C)

Preheat the grill to 225°F (107°C) for smoking. Put a disposable aluminum roasting pan under the grate to catch dripping juices.

On a cutting board, dry short ribs with paper towels.

Using a sharp chef's knife, cut any exterior fat off of meat side. Using a dry paper towel to grip, pull silver-skin (gristle) off underside. You may need a fork to get silverskin to start to curl up.

Rub yellow mustard followed by ½ cup Chipotle Rub into all parts of ribs, and place on a transport tray.

GRILLING TRIVIA

Beef short ribs can come in different forms and be called by different names. For example, a beef plate rib is a cut of three ribs cut just below the rib-eye, while a beef chuck rib is cut with four ribs and is the section above the brisket. Both of these types could also be purchased with the bones cut out. Boneless usually cook a bit faster, but they are not as flavorful.

1

Place short ribs meat side up on the grate over the drip pan for indirect cooking.

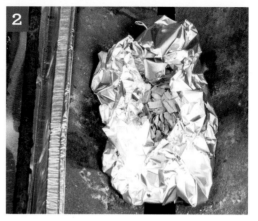

2

On a square of aluminum foil, place wood chips and roll up, leaving one end open. Put wrapped wood chips on the hot bed of the grill.

3 3 hours

Immediately cover the grill, and smoke for 3 hours, maintaining a temperature of 225°F (107°C) and not opening the grill.

4

Remove short ribs with tongs, and place on a sheet of aluminum foil. Sprinkle with remaining ½ cup Chipotle Rub, seal ribs into the foil, and return to the 225°F (107°C) grill for 2 hours.

5

Remove short ribs from the foil, and return to the 225°F (107°C) grill for 1 hour.

6

Remove short ribs from the grill, put on a cutting board, and let sit for 15 minutes to allow juices to rest.

7

Cut into 4-inch (10-cm) strips using a sharp chef's knife, place on a serving platter, and serve.

PORK

GRILL METHOD:
DIRECT HEAT

PREP TIME:
NONE

COOK TIME:
5-10 MIN.

SERVES: 4

Hot Dogs

Hot dogs are a kid-friendly favorite. Growing up, I would eat mine with a slice of American cheese and a bit of ketchup. You can buy 20 different kinds of these precooked sausages in the average grocery store consisting of different meat blends and spices, such as smokey links, traditional bratwurst, ring bologna, and cooked Italian links. This recipe shows how fast and easy they are to cook up for families on the go.

INGREDIENTS

8 hot dogs
8 hot dog buns
Condiments of your choice

TOOLS

Transport tray
Tongs
Squirt bottle filled with water

Meat thermometer
Serving platter

GRILL

1 | Medium

Preheat the grill to medium for direct-heat cooking. Make sure the grill is hot before you put hot dogs on the grate. Place hot dogs on a transport tray to take over to the grill.

2

Using tongs, place hot dogs on the hottest part of the grill over direct heat, making them parallel to the tines of the grill so they don't roll off, and allow to cook for 1 minute. If flames start to burn up from the bottom of the grill, give them a squirt of water with the squirt bottle.

3

Turn each hot dog ¼ turn, and cook for 1 minute. Keep doing this every minute until you›ve turned hot dogs completely.

4

Stick a meat thermometer into the end of a hot dog until it's to middle of meat, and see if it has reached an internal temperature of at least 165°F (74°C). If it hasn't, return to the grill. Repeat this process with other hot dogs.

5

When hot dogs reach the correct temperature, remove them from the grill, place them on buns, and place hot dogs on a serving platter. Serve with condiments of your choice.

PORK

GRILL METHOD:
DIRECT HEAT

PREP TIME:
15 MIN.

COOK TIME:
5 MIN.

SERVES: 2

Bratwursts

In the United States, "bratwurst" is a raw, uncooked sausage with a combination of meats and seasonings that have been ground together and stuffed into a casing. This recipe partially cooks the brats in a flavorful liquid: beer. Not only does this add some of the hops flavors from the beer, it also helps to seal the outside of the bratwurst so it doesn't break open as you cook it. You can also use this recipe for sausages similar to bratwurst.

CHEF'S TIP

There are a few reasons you need to steep a bratwurst before putting it directly onto the grill. The steeping process helps to soften the exterior so it expands as it cooks instead of blowing up. It also helps warm the bratwurst through so that when you put it on the hot grill, it will cook all the way through without burning by the time it gets to 165°F (74°C).

INGREDIENTS

2 local India pale ale (IPA)-style beers

2 uncooked bratwursts

2 Italian rolls, sliced open

Condiments of your choice

TOOLS

Pot (with heat-resistant handle) just big enough to hold bratwursts

Tongs

Squirt bottle filled with water

Meat thermometer

Serving platter

GRILL

High

Preheat the grill to high for direct-heat cooking. Put the pot on the grill, pour in India pale ale-style beers, and allow beer to come to a boil.

Add bratwursts. Remove the pot from the grill, and allow bratwursts to steep for 10 minutes.

Using tongs, place bratwursts on the hottest part of the grill over direct heat, parallel to the tines of the grill, and allow to cook for 2 minutes. If flames start to burn up from the bottom of the grill, give them a squirt of water with the squirt bottle.

Turn over bratwursts, and allow to cook for 2 minutes.

Stick your meat thermometer into the end of each bratwurst until it's at the middle of the meat. If the internal temperature isn't reading at least 165°F (74°C), return to the grill.

When bratwursts reach the correct temperature, remove from the grill, place on Italian rolls on a serving platter, and serve with condiments of your choice.

GRILL METHOD:
SMOKING

PREP TIME:
20 MIN.

COOK TIME:
4 HR.

SERVES: 4

Spareribs
with Kansas City Barbecue Sauce

Over the past several years, people have been brainwashed through advertising to think that baby back ribs are a superior cut over spareribs. However, I strongly believe that the spareribs are where the quality and value are located. The sparerib has more meat per bone than the baby back, and the cost of the sparerib is currently half that of baby backs. In this recipe, the pork flavor of the spareribs will shine through with the slight sweetness of the rub and will have a nice, smoky finish.

INGREDIENTS

2 (12-bone) pork sparerib racks

½ cup yellow mustard

1 cup Chipotle Rub (see "Seasonings and Condiments")

2 cups wood chips or smoking wood of your choice

1 cup Kansas City Barbecue Sauce (see "Seasonings and Condiments")

TOOLS

Disposable aluminum roasting pan

Paper towels

Cutting boards

Sharp chef's knife

Transport tray

Tongs

Aluminum foil

Sauce brush

Serving platter

PREP

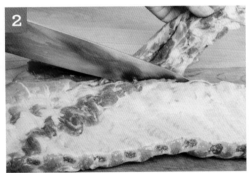

1 225°F (107°C)

Preheat the grill to 225°F (107°C) for smoking. Put a disposable aluminum roasting pan under the grate to catch dripping juices.

2 Dry spareribs with paper towels, and place on a cutting board. Using a sharp chef's knife, cut a straight line across top of bones, separating ribs from rib tips.

3 Using a dry paper towel to grip, pull silverskin (gristle) off underside of bones and rib tips. You may need a fork to get silverskin to start to curl up.

4 Rub yellow mustard all over spareribs.

5 Rub ½ cup Chipotle Rub onto ribs and tips. Put spareribs on a transport tray to take over to the grill.

Using tongs, place spareribs bone side down on the grate over the drip pan.

On a square of aluminum foil, place wood chips and roll up, leaving one end open. Put foil-covered wood chips on the hot bed of the grill.

2 hours

Immediately cover the grill, and smoke for 2 hours, maintaining a temperature of 225°F (107°C) and keeping the lid closed the entire time.

Open the grill, and set each rack of spareribs on a sheet of aluminum foil. Sprinkle with remaining ½ cup Chipotle Rub, and seal into the foil. Return to the grill still heated to 225°F (107°C) with the lid closed, and smoke for 1 hour.

5

Remove spareribs from the aluminum foil, and mop the ribs with the Kansas City Barbecue Sauce using a sauce brush. Return spareribs to the grill heated to 200°F (93°C), and smoke for 1 hour.

6

Remove spareribs from the grill, place on a cutting board, and allow to rest for 15 minutes. Cut between each bone, put on a serving platter, and serve with extra sauce.

GRILLING TRIVIA

The Kansas City Barbeque Society (kcbs.us) is the largest group of barbecue aficionados in the world. They have more than 15,000 members who compete in and judge over 400 sectioned competitions per year. The European countries have also started having competitions as well. And in Australia, there are days associated with bringing people together over barbecue.

GRILL METHOD:
SMOKING

PREP TIME:
20 MIN.

COOK TIME:
4 HR.

SERVES: 4

Baby Back Ribs
with Memphis Barbecue Sauce

Baby back ribs are sought after by many people for their small, easy-to-eat size. These ribs are each about 4 inches (10 cm) long, making it easier to eat around the bone compared to the longer sparerib bones. Because they are less meaty than spareribs, it also means that rubs and sauces for them need to be a bit lighter. This recipe is made with a Memphis rub and sauce, which leads to a smoky, slightly spicy rib balanced off with a sweet finish.

INGREDIENTS

2 (12-bone) pork baby back rib racks

1/2 cup yellow mustard

1 cup Memphis Barbecue Rub (see "Seasonings and Condiments")

2 cups wood chips or smoking wood of your choice

1 cup Memphis Barbecue Sauce (see "Seasonings and Condiments")

TOOLS

Disposable aluminum roasting pan

Cutting boards

Transport tray

Tongs

Aluminum foil

Sauce mop

Sharp chef's knife

Serving platter

PREP

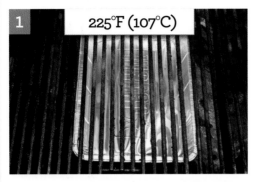

225°F (107°C)

Preheat the grill to 225°F (107°C) for smoking. Put a disposable aluminum roasting pan under the grate to catch dripping juices.

On a cutting board, pull silverskin (gristle) from back of ribs. Rub yellow mustard followed by ½ cup Memphis Barbecue Rub all over baby back ribs. Put baby back ribs on a transport tray.

GRILL

Place wood chips in aluminum foil, and lightly wrap. Put wrapped wood chips on the hot bed of the grill. Using tongs, place ribs bone side down on the grate over the drip pan, and smoke for 2 hours, maintaining a grill temperature of 225°F (107°C).

Set each rack of ribs on a sheet of aluminum foil, and sprinkle with remaining ½ cup Memphis Barbecue Rub. Seal baby back ribs into the foil, return to the grill still heated to 225°F (107°C), and smoke for 1 hour.

Remove baby back rib racks from the foil, and mop ribs with Memphis Barbecue Sauce using a sauce mop. Return baby back ribs to the grill heated to 200°F (93°C), and smoke for 1 hour.

Remove baby back ribs from the grill, place on a cutting board, and allow to rest for 15 minutes. Cut with a sharp chef's knife, put on a serving platter, and serve.

GRILL METHOD:
SMOKING

PREP TIME:
20 MIN.

COOK TIME:
14-16 HR.

SERVES: 10

PORK

Pulled Pork
with Carolina Barbecue Sauce

Pulled pork, which comes from the front shoulder of the pig, should be considered an art form unto itself. With every bite, you're made to think about the layers of flavors, the spices, and the sauces, which draws you in to take another bite. The shoulder has the most-used muscles of the pig, so you get something both flavorful and tough. To help with that toughness, this recipe shows you how to cook it for a long time at a low temperature to break down those connective tissues.

INGREDIENTS

1 (8- to 10-lb. [3.5- to 4.5-kg]) Boston roast

½ cup yellow mustard

1 cup Cajun Rub (see "Seasonings and Condiments")

2 cups wood chips or preferred smoke source

2 cups Carolina Barbecue Sauce (see "Seasonings and Condiments")

TOOLS

Transport tray

Paper towels

Disposable aluminum roasting pan

Tongs

In-oven meat thermometer

Aluminum foil

Rimless cookie sheet

Cutting board

Winter gloves

Extra-large rubber gloves

Serving platter

PREP

Put Boston roast skin side down on the transport tray, and dry with paper towels. Rub yellow mustard all over Boston roast.

Rub the Cajun Rub all over the rost. Put Boston roast into the refrigerator to stay cool while you prepare your grill or smoker.

CHEF'S TIP

I like to serve this as a sandwich with a little coleslaw on it, as the cool, acidic coleslaw is cleansing against the rich, hot pulled pork.

GRILL

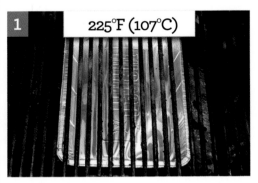

Preheat the grill to 225°F (107°C) for smoking. Put a disposable aluminum roasting pan under the grate to catch dripping juices.

Using tongs, place Boston roast skin/fat side down over the drip pan. Place an in-oven meat thermometer in thickest part of meat, making sure it isn't in fat between two muscles or next to bone.

3

Place wood chips in aluminum foil, and lightly wrap. Place wrapped wood chips on the heat source on each side of Boston roast.

4 14-16 hours

Immediately cover the grill, and smoke for 14 to 16 hours, maintaining a temperature of 225°F (107°C) and keeping the lid closed until the thermometer reaches 192°F (89°C).

5

Slide a rimless cookie sheet under Boston roast, and remove from the grill. Place Boston roast on a clean cutting board, and allow to rest for 15 minutes. Put on winter gloves, and then put on extra-large rubber gloves over them.

6

Follow the natural seams between muscles in Boston roast and separate them out, discarding connective tissue and fat.

Take muscles and shred to make pulled pork, keeping bark (outer crust) separate to make sure each of your guests gets a little bark.

If you're serving pulled pork "wet," add Carolina Barbecue Sauce to all of the meat except bark. (That should stay dry so it's crispy.). Put pulled pork on a serving platter, and serve.

GRILLING TRIVIA

In the 1700s, the better cuts of pork were packed into special barrels for shipment. These barrels were known as butts. The butchers in Boston had a unique way of cutting pork, so when the barrels were shipped, they were known as Boston butts. You can still find some places that refer to the front shoulder meat of the pig as the butt.

GRILL METHOD:
DIRECT HEAT

PREP TIME:
5 MIN.

COOK TIME:
10 MIN.

SERVES: 4

PORK

Pork Chops
with Peach Glaze

The days of grandma's old, dried-out hockey-puck pork chops are over. In the United States, the USDA has lowered the recommended cooking temperature of whole-muscle pork product from 160°F (71°C) to 145°F (63°C), which is significant when you learn that 65 percent of moisture is lost in lean meat when cooked to 160°F (71°C). This recipe is your chance to serve a juicy pork chop to your family using that new guideline, and in turn start teaching the next generation what pork should taste like. If your country's guidelines recommend a higher temperature, follow that; however, keep checking back, as more and more countries are using this new (and better) temperature.

INGREDIENTS

4 (½-lb. [226.75-g]) bone-in pork chops

2 TB. kosher salt

¼ TB. black pepper

¼ cup vegetable oil

1 cup Peach Glaze (see "Seasonings and Condiments")

TOOLS

Transport tray

Paper towel

Tongs

Squirt bottle filled with water

Meat thermometer

Sauce mop

Serving platter

PREP

1 Preheat the grill to medium for direct-heat cooking. Lay out pork chops on a transport tray, and blot dry with a paper towel. Season both sides of pork chops with kosher salt and black pepper.

2 Rub both sides of pork chops with vegetable oil to help conduct heat from the grill to chops.

GRILL

1 Using tongs, place pork chops on the hottest part of the grill over direct heat, and allow to cook for 2 minutes. If flames start to burn up from the bottom of the grill, use squirt bottle at flame's base.

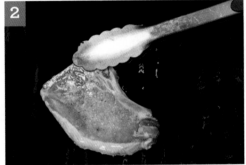

2 Rotate pork chops 45 degrees to make the cross-hatch pattern, and cook for 2 minutes. Flip pork chops, and repeat the process on the other side.

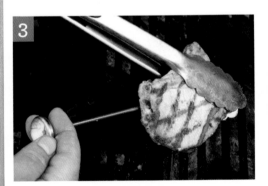

3 For each pork chop, put a meat thermometer in to check doneness, making sure at least 1 full inch (2.5 cm) of the thermometer stem is in meat. The desired internal temperature for pork chops is 145°F (63°C).

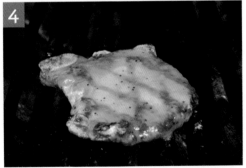

4 Brush both sides of pork chops with Peach Glaze using a sauce mop. Remove pork chops from the grill, place on a serving platter, and allow to rest for 5 minutes so juices redistribute evenly. Serve.

GRILL METHOD
INDIRECT HEAT

PREP TIME:
20 MIN.

COOK TIME:
1 HR.

SERVES: 10

Pork Roast
with Pesto

Unlike pork tenderloin, which is a small muscle usually weighing less than 1 pound (453.5 g), pork loin is a longer muscle that weighs at least 2 pounds (907 g) and is most known for being the main part of a pork chop. While pork loin is a less tender cut of meat than tenderloin, it's more meaty and flavorful. The recipe for this summer favorite shows you how to roast a pork loin on the grill and finish it with pesto. The sweet, nutty flavor of the pesto really gives the pork a fresh summer feel.

INGREDIENTS

1 (3-lb. [1.25-kg]) pork loin

3 TB. kosher salt

1 TB. black pepper

1 cup chicken stock (optional)

1 cup Pesto (see "Seasonings and Condiments")

TOOLS

Paper towels	In-oven meat thermometer
Cooling rack	Rimless cookie sheet
Sheet pan	Cutting board
Disposable aluminum roasting pan	Sharp slicing knife
Tongs	Serving platter

PREP

Dry pork loin with paper towels, and rub kosher salt and black pepper into all parts. Rub the pesto over the pork loin.

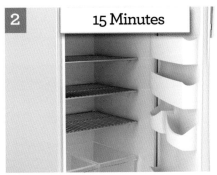

15 Minutes

Put a cooling rack on top of a sheet pan, and place pork loin fat side down onto the cooling rack. Place in the refrigerator to rest while you prep the grill. This allows the exterior of meat to dry out, which enables some of smoke flavor to penetrate into meat.

300°F (149°C)

Preheat the grill to 300°F (149°C) for indirect-heat cooking. Put a disposable aluminum roasting pan under the grate so it can catch dripping juices.

CHEF'S TIP

Leftovers make a great sandwich on crisp French bread.

HERITAGE BREEDS

For many years, the pork industry tried to breed all the fat out of pigs to make them lean for customers who were concerned about fat intake. What resulted was an extremely lean meat with little taste. This, in turn, may have caused some of your family recipes for pork to not turn out the same. However, growers have started going back to a more balanced fat content. If you can find meat from a heritage breed of pig, most of your pork recipes will taste and work better. The heritage breeds that are easiest to find are Berkshire, Duroc, and Mangalitsa.

GRILL

1

Using tongs, place pork loin fat side down on the grill over the drip pan. Place an in-oven meat thermometer in thickest part of meat.

2   1 hour

Cover the grill and cook for 1 hour, maintaining a temperature of 300°F (149°C) and not opening the grill again until the thermometer reaches 140°F (60°C).

3

Slide a rimless cookie sheet under pork roast, and remove from the grill. Place pork roast on a cutting board, and allow to rest on the cutting board for 15 minutes. During this time, the internal temperature will continue to climb to 145°F (63°C).

4

Remove the drip pan from the grill. Strain, degrease, and taste pan juices, or au jus. You can adjust the taste of au jus by adding kosher salt, black pepper, and chicken stock (if using) as needed.

On the cutting board, slice pork roast to your desired thickness across the grain using a sharp slicing knife.

Shingle pork roast slices on a serving platter, top with Pesto, and serve with au jus on the side.

STRAINING AND DEGREASING

Pan drippings are full of flavor that you won't want to miss out on. However, you'll want to remove the grease slick on top and strain out all the bigger bits first. To do this, follow these steps:

1. Put the pan drippings into a measuring cup.

2. Using a soup spoon, gently skim the oil that floats to the top and discard the oil.

3. Strain the remaining oil through a wire mesh strainer.

This will give you a resulting liquid that is cleaner and palatable.

GRILL METHOD:
INDIRECT HEAT

PREP TIME:
20 MIN. + 1 HR.

COOK TIME:
20 MIN.

SERVES: 2

Pork Tenderloin
with Asian Marinade

Marinating meat can do two things: add flavor, and tenderize the meat. Because this recipe is for cooking pork tenderloin, which is really tender, the included marinade is less acidic and used for flavor rather than tenderizing. The marinade balances the Asian flavors of salty, sweet, and spicy and uses the pork tenderloin as a canvas to paint them on.

INGREDIENTS

2 (1-lb. [453.5-g]) pork tenderloins

1 ½ cups Asian Marinade
(see "Seasonings and Condiments")

¼ cup vegetable oil

TOOLS

Cutting boards

Sharp slicing knife

Plastic zipper-lock bag

Paper towels

Disposable aluminum roasting pan

Tongs

In-oven meat thermometer

Serving platter

PREP

1 On a cutting board, remove silverskin (gristle) from pork tenderloin using a very sharp slicing knife, cutting under edge of silverskin and drawing the knife back against it to take off strips.

2 In a plastic zipper-lock bag, combine pork tenderloin pieces and ¾ cup Asian Marinade, squeezing out as much air as you can so marinade surrounds pork. Place in the refrigerator, and let marinate for 1 hour.

3 Remove from the refrigerator, and discard marinade and bag. Dry pork tenderloins with paper towels, and rub with vegetable oil.

400° F (204° C)

4 Preheat the grill to 400°F (204°C) for the indirect-heat cooking. Put a disposable aluminum roasting pan under the grate so it can catch dripping juices.

CHEF'S TIP

This dish is also wonderful served with peanut sauce.

GRILL

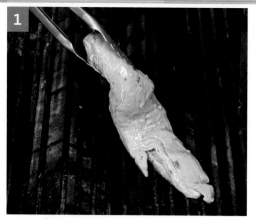

Using tongs, place pork tenderloin on the grate over the drip pan for indirect cooking. Place an in-oven meat thermometer in thickest part of thickest piece of meat.

20 minutes

Cover the grill, and cook for 20 minutes, maintaining a temperature of 400°F (204°C) and not opening the grill again until the thermometer reaches 140°F (60°C).

Remove pork tenderloin from the grill, place on a clean cutting board, and allow to rest for 15 minutes.

Pork tenderloin should now be a perfect medium-rare. Slice to your desired thickness across the grain, put onto a serving platter, and serve with remaining ¾ cup Asian Marinade.

DEMAND FOR PORK

Traditionally, Asian markets consumed very little meat. However, as they've started embracing the American culture, they've been eating a lot more animal products. Hogs are seen as number one in growth potential in Asia through 2020, which is causing pork prices to rise. Because of these higher prices, you may want to consider using pork loin in this recipe instead of pork tenderloin.

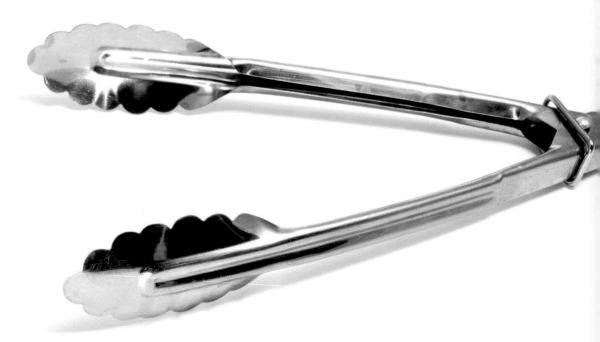

GRILL METHOD:
DIRECT HEAT

PREP TIME:
5 MIN.

COOK TIME:
10 MIN.

SERVES: 4

PORK

Ground Pork
with Sun-Dried Tomato Ketchup

Using ground pork as the meat for a burger means you're starting with much more complex flavors than beef. In place of traditional ketchup, which has acid levels pork can't stand up to, this recipe includes a ketchup made from sun-dried tomatoes. This ketchup gives a hint of citrus fruit from the tomatoes for the acid but cuts way back on the normal vinegar. In the end, you have a more approachable burger with nuances of the Mediterranean.

CHEF'S TIP

When working meat for a burger, don't mix it too much. The more it's mixed, the tougher it becomes.

INGREDIENTS

2 lb. (907 g) ground pork

1 TB. kosher salt

¼ TB. black pepper

¼ cup vegetable oil

4 Asiago cheese buns

½ cup Sun-Dried Tomato Ketchup
 (see "Seasonings and Condiments")

TOOLS

Mixing bowl

Transport tray

Tongs

Squirt bottle filled with water

Meat thermometer

Serving platter

PREP

1 Medium

Preheat the grill to medium for direct-heat cooking.

2

In a large mixing bowl, combine ground pork, kosher salt, and black pepper. Mold patties a little bit bigger than the bun, rub both sides with vegetable oil, and place on a transport tray.

GRILL

1

Using tongs, place pork patties on the hottest part of the grill over direct heat, and allow to cook for 2 minutes. If flames start to burn up from the bottom of the grill, use squirt bottle at flame's base.

2

Rotate pork burgers 45 degrees to make the cross-hatch pattern, and cook for 2 more minutes. Flip burgers, and repeat the process on the other side.

3

Put a meat thermometer into burger to check doneness, making sure that at least 1 full inch (2.5 cm) of the thermometer stem is in meat. The desired internal temperature for pork is 140°F (60°C).

4

Remove pork burgers from the grill, and place onto Asiago cheese buns. Add 2 tablespoons Sun-Dried Tomato Ketchup to each burger, place burgers on a serving platter, and serve.

GRILL METHOD:
INDIRECT HEAT

PREP TIME:
10 MIN. + 1 HR.

COOK TIME:
10 MIN.

SERVES: 12

Pork Belly
with Thai Sauce

Grilled bacon is very popular in many Asian cultures. As I traveled through Singapore, I was shocked to see the street businesses that specialized in this bacon. Try to find bacon that hasn't been cured and is still in one slab; this will give you more flexibility in how long you can marinate the meat. If all you can find is cured bacon, get the thickest slices you can find.

INGREDIENTS

1 lb. (453.5 g) pork belly, skin on and cut into ¼-in.-thick×4-in.-long (.5-cm-thick×10-cm-long) pieces

1 cup Asian Marinade (see "Seasonings and Condiments")

½ cup Thai Sauce (see "Seasonings and Condiments")

TOOLS

Plastic zipper-lock bag

Paper towels

Disposable aluminum roasting pan

Tongs

Mesh wire grilling rack

Squirt bottle filled with water

Sauce ramekins

Serving platter

PREP

In a plastic zipper-lock bag, combine pork belly and Asian Marinade, squeezing the air out of the bag so marinade is completely around pork belly. Place in the refrigerator, and allow to marinate for 1 hour. (If you're using cured bacon, marinate for only 20 minutes.)

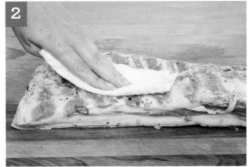

Remove from the refrigerator, and discard marinade and bag. Pat pork belly dry with paper towels.

CHEF'S TIP

Make sure you follow the steps closely, as the meat could burn quickly from dripping grease if you don't do so.

GRILL

400° F (204° C)

Preheat the grill to 400°F (204°C) for indirect-heat cooking. Put a disposable aluminum roasting pan under the grate so it can catch dripping juices.

Place pork belly pieces over the drip pan.

Cover the grill, and allow the temperature of the grill to recover to 400°F (204°C). Open the grill, and turn pork belly pieces.

400° F (204° C)

Cover the grill again, and allow the temperature to recover to 400°F (204°C).

Using two pairs of tongs, move pork bacon and mesh wire grilling rack over direct heat. At this point, most of the grease should be rendered out, so there's less likelihood of flare-ups.

Turn pork bacon every 30 seconds until it's crunchy, being careful not to burn it. Have the squirt bottle ready to drench any grease fires that may flare up. Cut up pork bacon into small pieces and place them on a serving platter. Pour Thai Sauce into sauce ramekins, place on the serving platter, and serve.

FINDING BARGAINS FOR BACON

Bacon prices have been skyrocketing in the past few years. If you can find jowl meat, it actually works much better in the recipe and is about half the price.

GRILL METHOD:
DIRECT HEAT

PREP TIME:
20 MIN. + 4 HR.

COOK TIME:
10 MIN.

SERVES: 12

Lamb Kebabs
with Curry Rub

Lamb is an often-overlooked meat. The way lamb is raised today, it doesn't have the strong, gamey flavors it used to have. This recipe is for a Middle-Eastern inspired lamb kebab. The yogurt marinade helps to start making the tough meat a bit more tender and adds a rich, acidic flavor that helps tame the meat. The curry rub melts into the yogurt to give the finished grilled lamb a rich, earthy flavor that will make your mouth water.

INGREDIENTS

2 cups Athenian Marinade (see "Seasonings and Condiments")

¼ cup Curry Rub (see "Seasonings and Condiments")

1 ½ lb. (680 g) lamb shoulder, cut into a 1-in. (2.5-cm) dice

TOOLS

Plastic zipper-lock bag

Good-quality meat skewers or wooden skewers soaked in water

Transport tray

Serving platter

PREP

If you're using lamb that's already marinated, skip to Grill 1.

1

In a plastic bag, combine Athenian Marinade and Curry Rub, mixing completely.

2

Add lamb to bag. Squeeze out as much air as possible, and seal the bag. Put bag into the refrigerator, and allow to marinate for 4 hours.

3

Remove lamb from the plastic bag, and divide evenly among 4 good-quality skewers. Leave at least ¼ inch (.5 cm) between each lamb piece so pieces in the middle can cook. If you're using wooden skewers, put 2 skewers through each piece of meat; this will make them much easier to turn while they are cooking.

4

Put lamb kebabs on a transport tray. Don't use an aluminum pan or foil to do this, as acids in yogurt will start to eat into the aluminum.

CHEF'S TIP

Grilling lamb is a very easy way to upscale your menu and increase your nutrition, so check out your choices the next time you're walking by the meat case. Many times, the meat is already marinated and ready to grill as soon as you get home. Three ounces of lean cook lamb contains 43 percent of the protein, 74 percent of the vitamin B$_{12}$, and 30 percent of the zinc you need daily. Most of the fat on lamb is on the exterior instead of in the marbling, meaning it's much easier than most meats to just cut off the fat and not consume it. Doing this will greatly reduce your saturated fat intake.

GRILL

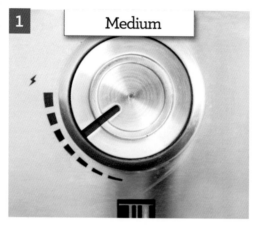

Medium

Preheat the grill to medium for direct-heat cooking.

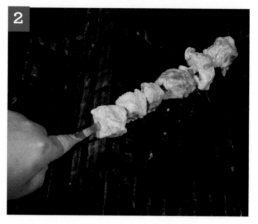

Place lamb kebabs on the grill over direct heat, and allow to cook for 2 minutes on each side.

As you turn lamb, brush the grill grate where lamb kebabs were before. This keeps yogurt from burning on the grate and giving lamb a burnt smell.

After all four sides of lamb kebabs have cooked, cut a kebab open to check for doneness. Inside of kebab should be medium-rare (or your personal preference).

5

Remove lamb kebabs from the grill, place on a serving platter, and serve over rice with additional grilled vegetables.

SKEWERS AND SKEWERING FOODS

Not all skewers are created equal. Ideally, use heavyweight skewers that look somewhat like miniature swords. With a blade-shaped skewer, the skewered item is less likely to flop around. Metal skewers are also nice, because they help conduct heat through the middle, where it's sometimes hard to get everything cooked. If you use wooden skewers, soaking them in water before using them is a must; otherwise, they will catch fire.

When it comes to skewering foods, don't be tempted to put vegetables on the same skewers as meat. Vegetables and meat cook at different speeds, so by the time the meat is done, the veggies are burned. Make a separate skewer for each item and, after they're cooked, you can serve them one of two ways: take them off the skewers and serve over rice, or alternate the meat and vegetable skewers on the platter and allow your guests to remove the food from the skewers themselves.

GRILL METHOD
DIRECT HEAT

PREP TIME:
5 MIN.

COOK TIME:
8MIN.

SERVES: 4

Ground Lamb
with Thai Sauce

Ginger, garlic, and green onions really bring out the flavors in ground lamb and are the classic base flavors of most Asian foods. This ground lamb burger builds layers of flavors that resemble a Korean Bahn Mi sandwich. For this recipe, I also like to add a couple of chile peppers to this to spice it up. If you like a richer flavor, look for meat that's from New Zealand- or Australian-raised animals. Finishing the food with a Thai sauce adds that last layer of the ginger, garlic, and green onion flavor plus a rich, savory component that brings all the ingredients together.

INGREDIENTS

1 ½ lb. (680 g) ground lamb

1 tsp. chopped garlic

1 tsp. fresh ground ginger

1 tsp. minced green onion

1 TB. kosher salt

¼ cup vegetable oil

½ cup Thai Sauce (see "Seasonings and Condiments")

4 firm hamburger buns

1 cup fresh cilantro leaves

TOOLS

Mixing bowl

Transport tray

Tongs

Squirt bottle filled with water

Meat thermometer

Sauce brush

Serving platter

PREP

Preheat the grill to medium for direct-heat cooking. In a large mixing bowl, combine lamb, garlic, ginger, green onion, and kosher salt. Divide lamb patty mixture into 4 burgers the same width as your buns.

Rub down lamb patties with vegetable oil so it's evenly dispersed, and place on a transport tray.

GRILL

Using tongs, place lamb patties on the hottest part of the grill over direct heat, and allow to cook for 2 minutes. If flames start to burn up from the bottom of the grill, use the squirt bottle.

Rotate lamb patties 45 degrees on the same side to create the cross-hatch pattern, and cook for another 2 minutes. Flip lamb patties, and repeat the process on the other side.

Put a meat thermometer into a patty to check doneness, making sure at least 1 full inch (2.5 cm) of the thermometer stem is in meat.

When the thermometer reaches 162°F (72°C), brush both sides of patties with Thai Sauce using a sauce brush. Remove from the grill, place on hamburger buns on a serving platter, and allow to rest for 5 minutes. Top lamb burgers with cilantro, and serve.

GRILL METHOD:
DIRECT HEAT

PREP TIME:
5 MIN.

COOK TIME:
8 MIN.

SERVES: 4

Lamb Chops
with Garlic-Herb Compound Butter

When looking for a lamb "chop," you can get a rib rack and cut it into steaks, or you can buy lamb loin chops. The latter are like little porterhouse steaks from a sheep. The bone going through the middle and end of the meat helps to add flavor to the meat as it cooks. American-raised loin chops are less gamey and a bit larger, while European and Australian lamb is more richly flavored and preferred by many diners. In this recipe for lamb chops, the compound butter added in the end will melt and add a wonderful garlic and herb lusciousness. The USDA suggests that lamb should be cooked to a minimum of 145°F (63°C); I recommend taking them off at 140°F (60°C) and allowing them to carryover cook to reach the final 5° (3°).

INGREDIENTS

8 (between 3 and 5 oz. [85 and 142 g] each) bone-in lamb loin chops

2 TB. kosher salt

¼ TB. black pepper

¼ cup vegetable oil

4 TB. Garlic-Herb Compound Butter (see "Seasonings and Condiments")

TOOLS

Paper towel

Transport tray

Tongs

Squirt bottle filled with water

Meat thermometer

Serving platter

PREP

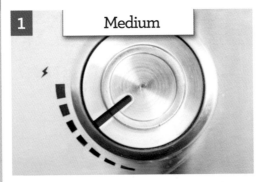

Medium

Preheat the grill to medium for direct-heat cooking. Blot lamb loin chops dry with a paper towel, and season both sides with kosher salt and black pepper.

Rub lamb loin chops evenly with vegetable oil.

GRILL

Using tongs, place lamb loin chops on the hottest part of the grill over direct heat, and allow to cook for 2 minutes. If flames start up from oils, douse with a squirt of water from the squirt bottle.

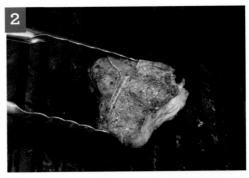

Rotate chops 45 degrees on the same side to make the cross-hatch pattern, and cook for 2 minutes. Flip lamb loin chops, and repeat the process on the other side.

Put a meat thermometer into a chop, making sure at least 1 full inch (2.5 cm) of the thermometer stem is in meat and not next to the bone.

When the desired temperature is reached, remove lamb loin chops from the grill and onto a serving platter, and allow to rest for 5 minutes. Top each lamb loin chop with Garlic-Herb Compound Butter, and serve.

GRILL METHOD:
INDIRECT HEAT

PREP TIME:
45 MIN.

COOK TIME:
15 MIN.

SERVES: 4

Rack of Lamb
with Papaya-Mint Salsa

Sweet mint jelly was served with lamb because lamb used to be extremely gamey, and the sugar and mint helped cover up the flavor of the meat. The industry has come a long way in raising and slaughtering sheep for maximum flavor, but if you have to have mint with lamb, give it a new look with some mint-flavored salsa. By using the salsa in this recipe, you give a nod to the classics but let the delicate flavors of the meat shine.

INGREDIENTS

4 stems fresh rosemary

3 TB. kosher salt

1 TB. black pepper

2 racks lamb (8 bones on a rack)

1 cup Papaya-Mint Salsa (see "Seasonings and Condiments")

TOOLS

Mixing bowl

Cutting boards

Sharp boning knife

Aluminum foil

Sheet pan

Disposable aluminum roasting pan

Tongs

In-oven meat thermometer

Sharp slicing knife

Serving platter

Meat fork

PREP

Remove leaves from 1 rosemary stem and mince finely. In a small mixing bowl, combine minced rosemary from 1 stem, kosher salt, and black pepper, and mix well.

On a cutting board, cut outer layer of fat off of lamb racks. A thin layer of meat must be cut out to get out all the fat.

Cut fat and connective tissue from between each lamb bone using a sharp boning knife. Get as close as you can to each bone, fold membrane back to meat, and cut at base of bone.

Using the back of the boning knife, scrape any remaining tissue off every lamb bone. Any bits left over will burn onto lamb bone when cooked.

Cover lamb bones with aluminum foil to help keep them white, and place on a sheet pan.

Season lamb on all sides with seasoning mixture.

GRILL

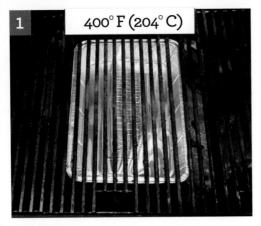

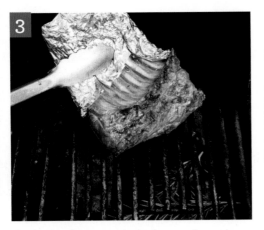

400° F (204° C)

Preheat the grill to 400°F (204°C) for indirect-heat cooking. Put a disposable aluminum roasting pan under the grate.

Add remaining 3 rosemary stems directly to the heat source. Using tongs, place meat of lamb rack on the grate over direct heat, with bones hanging over the aluminum pan. Let meat cook for 2 minutes to develop browning.

Turn lamb racks so uncooked side is now facing the heat source and bones are once again over the aluminum pan, and cook for 2 minutes.

Move entire lamb racks over the aluminum pan. Put an in-oven meat thermometer in the middle of largest piece, and close the lid.

Once lamb racks have reached an internal temperature of 140°F (60°C), about 10 minutes, remove from the grill to a clean cutting board, and allow to rest for 15 minutes.

Lamb meat should be a perfect medium-rare. Slice between each rib with a sharp slicing knife, place on a serving platter with meat fork for pickup, and serve with Papaya-Mint Salsa.

THE TEST OF A CHEF

Some people may ask, "Why clean the bones and cover them with foil?" There are a couple of reasons. First, if they aren't covered, they could hang between the grate and start to burn when close to the flame. The bigger reason for a chef to do this, though, is to show the quality of preparation. The more you can get all the little meat and fat pieces removed, the more you show that you have taken time to treat the meat correctly. And the whiteness of the bone tells the person eating the meat the food is of high-quality preparation.

123

GRILL METHOD:
INDIRECT HEAT

PREP TIME:
20 MIN. + 24 HR.

COOK TIME:
2 HR.

SERVES: 12

LAMB

Leg of Lamb
with Orange-Ale Marinade

Leg of lamb is not nearly as tough as beef or pork. Especially with the top half of the leg, it could be roasted to rare and enjoyed. In fact, Australians claim roasted legs of lamb as their national dish and simply roast the leg at close to 400°F (204°C) for an hour. This recipe adds a layer of flavor with a marinade that brings out the citrus character in grass-fed lamb. And of course, the ale accents the beverage of choice for grilling out.

INGREDIENTS

4 TB. kosher salt

1 TB. black pepper

1 tsp. fresh rosemary, minced

1 (about 6- to 7-lb. [2.75- to 3-kg]) lamb leg, boned

½ cup wood chips

2 cups beef stock (optional)

4 cups Orange-Ale Marinade (see "Seasonings and Condiments")

TOOLS

Mixing bowl

Paper towel

Sheet pan

Large plastic zipper-lock bag

Disposable aluminum roasting pan

Tongs

In-oven meat thermometer

Aluminum foil

Rimless cookie sheet

Cutting board

Sharp slicing knife

Serving platter

Meat fork

Sauce ramekins

In a small mixing bowl, combine kosher salt, black pepper, and rosemary, and mix well.

Dry leg of lamb with paper towels, and place on a sheet pan. Untie leg of lamb, roll open, and rub seasoning mixture into all parts of lamb meat.

In a large plastic zipper-lock bag, place lamb and enough Orange-Ale Marinade to cover meat when all the air is pushed out of the bag, and seal the bag.

24 Hours

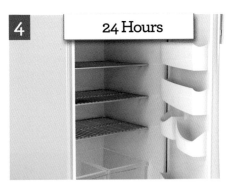

Place bag of lamb meat in the refrigerator, and allow to marinate for 24 hours.

350°F (177°C)

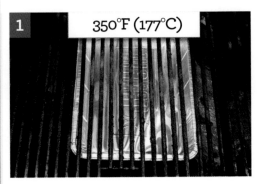

Preheat the grill to hold at 350°F (177°C) for indirect-heat cooking. Place a disposable aluminum roasting pan under the grate to catch dripping juices.

Using tongs, place leg of lamb fat side down on the grate over the drip pan, and put an in-oven meat thermometer in thickest part of meat.

Place wood chips in aluminum foil and roll up, leaving one end open. Place wrapped wood chips on the heat source.

2 hours

Cover the grill, and cook for 2 hours, maintaining a temperature of 350°F (177°C) and not opening the grill until the thermometer says lamb has reached an internal temperature of 135°F (57°C).

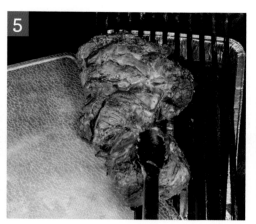

Slide a rimless cookie sheet under leg of lamb, and remove from the grill. Put leg of lamb on a clean cutting board, and allow to rest for 15 minutes.

Remove the aluminum roasting pan from the grill. Strain, degrease, and taste pan juices (also known as au jus), adjusting taste by adding kosher salt, black pepper, and beef stock (if using) as needed.

7

Using a sharp slicing knife, slice leg of lamb to your desired thickness across the grain. Put leg of lamb on a serving platter with a meat fork for pickup, pour au jus into sauce ramekins, and serve.

BUYING LAMB

Sometimes there are so many things to try and figure out when buying lamb, it can become paralyzing. Here are some terms you might see associated with lamb and what they mean.

Halal	The lamb was slaughtered by a Muslim and was alive at time of slaughter. The lamb was also bled out entirely.
Kosher	The lamb was slaughtered by an ordained Jew and was alive at the time of the slaughter. It was also allowed to bleed out entirely. Only the forequarter of the lamb is considered kosher.
Grass-finished (different from grass-fed, which is how almost all lamb starts out)	This animal fed on grass its entire life, making the resulting meat more gamey. This term applies to most lamb grown in Australia and New Zealand.
Grain-finished	The lamb was likely fed on pasture for the first few months of its life and then brought onto a feed lot to be fed a diet rich in grains. The grains make the meat less gamey and increase the body size of the animal rather quickly. This is the process used primarily in the United States.

POULTRY

How to Cut Up a Whole Chicken

Once you've learned how easy it is to cut a whole chicken into pieces, you'll never go back to buying the cut-up stuff again. When you cut your own chicken, you also have the leftover bones to use for stock, a foundation for so many sauces and soups. But the biggest difference you'll notice is the price—a whole chicken costs significantly less per pound than precut chicken parts. When I buy whole chickens, I usually get several, cut them down, and freeze them by cut.

INGREDIENTS

1 whole chicken, any
  size

TOOLS

Cutting board
Sharp boning knife

Place chicken on a cutting board back side down, with the neck pointing toward you.

Using a sharp boning knife, slice down the top-middle of the breast until you reach the bone. Follow the bone down and to the side, cutting under the breast meat. Follow the wishbone to where the wing attaches to the body.

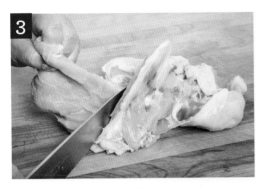

Cut through the cartilage of the wing-body joint, and cut the skin between the thigh and the breast to free the breast. Put the breast aside and repeat the process on the other side of the breast.

Turn chicken around so the leg is pointing toward you. Down near the base of the thigh, you should feel the hip joint. Cut behind that thigh meat and in front of the hip bone to expose the joint.

Follow the outside of the body cavity around to the thigh-body joint. Cut through that joint to release the dark meat from the body. Put the dark meat aside and repeat the process for the other side.

Move the thigh-leg quarters to the cutting board. Find the thin line of fat right above the joint, and cut straight down through it. Your knife should come down cleanly between the bones. Repeat this for the other thigh-leg quarter. Move these finished pieces aside.

Move the breast quarters back to the cutting board skin side up, and cut around the breast where the wing joint is attached. Repeat this process with the other breast-wing quarter.

You should now have the basic 8-piece cuts of chicken. Freeze chicken pieces, and make stock with the body frame.

GRILL METHOD:
DIRECT HEAT

PREP TIME:
5 MIN.

COOK TIME:
4 MIN.

SERVES: 4

Basic Chicken Breasts

Once you have the idea of how to do the basic grilled chicken breast, it's easy to spice things up by adding different seasonings and rubs, or finishing it with different sauces and salsas. This recipe uses boneless, skin-on breasts. I recommend using skin-on breasts to cook with, even if you discard the skin after it's cooked, because the fats in the skin are what burn and create that distinctive grilled flavor.

CHEF'S TIP

You can also try this recipe with bone-in chicken breasts, which will have a meatier flavor after being grilled.

INGREDIENTS

4 (6-oz. [170-g]) chicken breasts, boneless and skin on

2 TB. kosher salt

¼ TB. black pepper

¼ cup vegetable oil

TOOLS

Transport tray

Paper towel

Tongs

Squirt bottle filled with water

Meat thermometer

Serving platter

PREP

Medium-High

Preheat the grill to medium-high for direct-heat cooking.

Place chicken breasts on a transport tray, and dry with a paper towel. Liberally season with kosher salt and black pepper, and rub down with vegetable oil.

GRILL

Using tongs, place chicken breasts skin side down on the grill over direct heat, and allow to cook for 1 minute. If flames start to burn up from the bottom of the grill, give them a squirt of water with the squirt bottle.

Pick up each breast with the tongs, rotate 45 degrees to make the cross-hatch pattern, and cook for 1 minute. If chicken sticks to the grill as you're trying to do this, wait another minute before rotating.

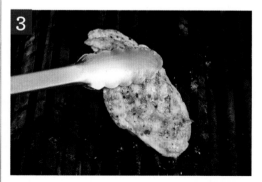

Flip chicken breasts, and repeat the process on the other side. Put a meat thermometer in each breast to check doneness, making sure at least 1 full inch (2.5 cm) of the thermometer stem is in thickest part of meat.

When it reaches 165°F (74°C), remove chicken breasts from the grill, place on a serving platter, and allow to rest for 5 minutes. Serve.

POULTRY

GRILL METHOD:
DIRECT HEAT

PREP TIME:
30 MIN.

COOK TIME:
10 MIN.

SERVES: 4

Chicken Breast
with Citrus-Fennel Marinade

Chicken and citrus are often paired together, because chicken has a natural sweetness that's accented well by the citrus aroma. This recipe includes a marinade with citrus as well as fennel that adds a background of licorice. You can follow this recipe as a guideline and substitute any marinade.

INGREDIENTS

4 (6-oz. [170-g]) chicken breasts, bone in and skin on

1 cup Citrus-Fennel Marinade (see "Seasonings and Condiments")

¼ cup vegetable oil

2 oranges, peeled, segments only

2 TB. chopped green tops from fresh fennel bulb

TOOLS

Plastic zipper-lock bag

Transport tray

Tongs

Squirt bottle filled with water

Meat thermometer

Serving platter

PREP

1 Put chicken breasts and Citrus-Fennel Marinade in a plastic zipper-lock bag, squeeze as much air out of the bag as you can, and seal the top. Place the bag in the refrigerator, and allow to marinate for 20 minutes.

2 Remove chicken from the bag, put skin side up on a transport tray, and wipe all the excess marinade off so exterior is dry.

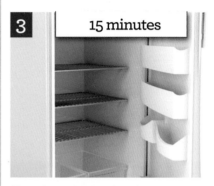

3 | 15 minutes

Place chicken back in the refrigerator, and allow to rest while you prep the grill. This allows exterior of meat to dry out, which makes chicken skin crisp up when cooked.

4 | Medium

Preheat the grill to medium for direct-heat cooking.

CHEF'S TIP

Chicken is a blank canvas that can be paired with different marinades. Salty marinades in particular do a great job of keeping chicken moist as it cooks. However, don't buy chicken to marinate if it says it has been "packed in water" or "10% brine solution added." The resulting chicken will be extremely salty.

Rub chicken with vegetable oil. Using tongs, place chicken skin side down on the grill over direct heat, and allow to cook for 2 minutes. If flames start to burn up from the bottom of the grill, give them a squirt of water with the squirt bottle.

Pick up each chicken breast with the tongs, rotate 45 degrees to make the cross-hatch pattern, and cook for 2 minutes. If chicken sticks to the grill as you're trying to do this, just wait another minute before rotating.

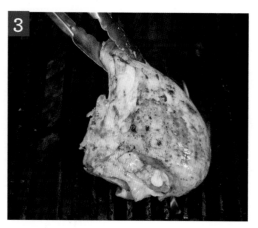

Flip chicken breasts bone side down, and allow to cook for 6 minutes.

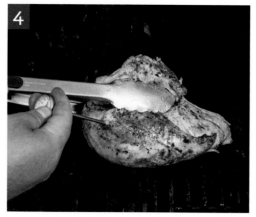

Put a meat thermometer in each breast to check doneness. When the internal temperature reaches 160°F (71°C), remove chicken from the grill, place on a serving platter, and allow to rest for 5 minutes.

5 Serve garnished with orange segments and chopped fennel tops.

GROCERY-STORE VS. HERITAGE-BREED CHICKENS

You can find many different kinds of chicken with different flavors and nutritional value in grocery stores today. The average grocery store chicken is a breed that was developed to grow quickly and to have a big, meaty breast. They're usually not raised in an area where they have fresh ground to peck at, so they don't taste as "chicken-y" as heritage-breed chickens that are raised primarily outdoors. When a chicken is raised outdoors with fresh ground to peck at on a normal basis, the meat is much more yellow, because the fats are much higher in omega-3 fatty acids. Try using heritage-breed chicken meat, as these chickens have more flavor and are healthier than the others, though the size of the breast may be less than what you're accustomed to. You can find heritage-breed chickens at a specialty grocer or a farmers' market.

GRILL METHOD:
SMOKING

PREP TIME:
5 MIN.

COOK TIME:
20 MIN.

SERVES: 4

POULTRY

Chicken Legs
with Alabama Barbecue Sauce

Dark meat has more flavor than white meat and holds moisture better, which makes dark chicken meat better suited for smoking. In this recipe, I smoke the legs and serve them with a mayonnaise-based barbecue sauce; the sauce provides a tangy flavor with a big kick of black pepper.

CHEF'S TIP

Keeping the grill closed helps to develop the smoky flavors and appearance.

INGREDIENTS

8 chicken legs, any size

2 TB. kosher salt

¼ TB. black pepper

2 cups wood chips or preferred smoke source

1 cup Alabama Barbecue Sauce (see "Seasonings and Condiments")

TOOLS

Cutting board

Paper towel

Transport tray

Disposable aluminum roasting pan

Tongs

In-oven meat thermometer

Aluminum foil

Serving platter

PREP

On a cutting board, dry chicken legs with a paper towel, and season with kosher salt and black pepper. Put in the refrigerator on a transport tray, uncovered, until the grill is ready.

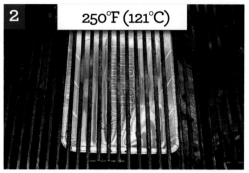

250°F (121°C)

Preheat the grill to 250°F (121°C) for smoking. Put a disposable aluminum roasting pan under the grate so it can catch dripping juices.

GRILL

Using tongs, place chicken legs on the grate over roasting pan. Place an in-oven meat thermometer in thickest part of meat, making sure it isn't touching bone.

On a square of aluminum foil, place wood chips and roll up, leaving one end open. Put wood chips on the heat source.

20 minutes

Immediately cover the grill, and smoke for 20 minutes, maintaining a temperature of 250°F (121°C) and not opening the grill again until the thermometer reaches 165°F (74°C).

Remove from the grill, place on a serving platter, and allow to rest for 15 minutes. Cover with Alabama Barbecue Sauce, and serve.

GRILL METHOD:
SMOKING

PREP TIME:
5 MIN.

COOK TIME:
20 MIN.

SERVES: 4

POULTRY

Chicken Thighs
with Kansas City Barbecue Sauce

This recipe is how you would see a typical barbecue competition team prepare their chicken. Chicken thighs have nice flavor and a consistent look, plus they can be cooked up in large batches and reheated quickly. This makes them great for parties and family get-togethers.

INGREDIENTS

8 chicken thighs, any size

1 cup Memphis Barbecue Rub (see "Seasonings and Condiments")

2 cups wood chips or preferred smoke source

1 cup Kansas City Barbecue Sauce (see "Seasonings and Condiments")

TOOLS

Cutting board

Paper towel

Transport tray

Disposable aluminum roasting pan

Tongs

In-oven meat thermometer

Aluminum foil

Serving platter

PREP

On a cutting board, dry chicken thighs with a paper towel, and coat with Memphis Barbecue Rub. Put in the refrigerator on a transport tray, uncovered, until the grill is ready.

250°F (121°C)

Preheat the grill to 250°F (121°C) for smoking. Put a disposable aluminum roasting pan under the grate so it can catch dripping juices.

GRILL

Using tongs, place chicken thighs on the grate over a drip pan. Place an in-oven meat thermometer in thickest part of meat, making sure it isn't touching bone.

On a square of aluminum foil, place wood chips and roll up, leaving one end open. Put wrapped wood chips on the heat source.

20 minutes

Immediately cover the grill, and smoke for 20 minutes, maintaining a temperature of 250°F (121°C) and not opening the grill again until the thermometer reaches 165°F (74°C).

Remove chicken thighs from the grill, place on a serving platter, and allow to rest for 15 minutes. Cover with Kansas City Barbecue Sauce, and serve.

GRILL METHOD:
SMOKING

PREP TIME:
30 MIN.

COOK TIME:
30 MIN.

SERVES: 4

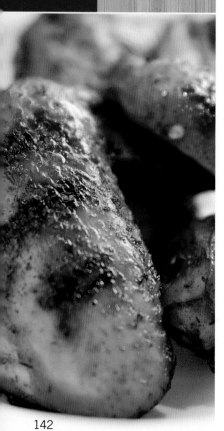

Chicken Wings
with Jamaican Jerk Rub

Jerk chicken is the national dish of Jamaica. The technique was brought to the island by the Maroons, who used indigenous Jamaican foods combined with African cooking techniques. Traditionally, jerk chicken is made using whole chicken. However, jerk style has become a popular way of eating chicken wings, which is what this recipe uses; combined with the rub, these spicy wings need a good beer to help wash away the heat.

INGREDIENTS

12 chicken wings, any size, all three sections attached

2 cups Jamaican Jerk Rub (see "Seasonings and Condiments")

2 cups wood chips or preferred smoke source

TOOLS

Paper towel

Plastic zipper-lock bag

Transport tray

Disposable aluminum roasting pan

Tongs

Aluminum foil

Serving platter

142

PREP

1 Dry chicken wings with a paper towel. Put wings into a plastic zipper-lock bag, and add 1 cup Jamaican Jerk Rub to the bag. Squeeze as much air out of the bag as possible, seal, and place in the refrigerator to marinate for at least 20 minutes.

2 250°F (121°C)

Preheat the grill to 250°F (121°C) for smoking. Put a disposable aluminum roasting pan under the grate so it can catch dripping juices. Remove chicken wings from the refrigerator, take out of bag, and place on a transport tray.

GRILL

1 Using tongs, place chicken thighs on the grate over the roasting pan. Make sure wings aren't touching each other so the smoke can reach all around meat.

2 On a square of aluminum foil, place wood chips and roll up, leaving one end open. Put wrapped wood chips on the heat source.

3 30 minutes

Immediately cover the grill, and smoke for 30 minutes, maintaining a temperature of 250°F (121°C) and not opening the grill until that time has passed.

4 Remove wings from the grill, and place on a serving platter. Cover with remaining 1 cup Jamaican Jerk Rub, and serve.

GRILL METHOD:
INDIRECT HEAT

PREP TIME:
10 MIN. + 12 HR.

COOK TIME:
1 HR.

SERVES: 4

Whole Chicken
with Mediterranean Rub

A basic roast chicken is the one thing I think all good cooks should be able to do well. Indirect-heat cooking on the grill is a rustic form of roasting that will add additional flavor to the chicken. It's so simple in concept, but not so easy to achieve the perfect result. It can be broken down to four simple steps: season, roast, rest, and serve. The hard part is all the balancing that has to happen. You have to have the right amount of seasoning without overpowering the flavor of the chicken. You have to have the right amount of dry heat to crisp the skin, but not so much that the skin burns before the inside is done. You have to let the chicken rest long enough for the juices to redistribute evenly, but not so long that the chicken is cold. Patience is the key.

INGREDIENTS

1 (5- to 6-lb. [2.25- to 2.75-kg]) whole chicken

¼ cup Mediterranean Rub (see "Seasonings and Condiments")

½ cup wood chips

1 cup chicken stock (optional)

TOOLS

Disposable aluminum roasting pan

Cooling rack

Rimmed sheet pan

Tongs

Aluminum foil

In-oven meat thermometer

Serving platter

PREP

1

Remove giblets and neck from body cavity of chicken, and put inside the disposable aluminum roasting pan while setting up the grill. Dry chicken with paper towels, and rub Mediterranean Rub into all parts of chicken (not forgetting the inside).

2

Put a cooling rack on top of a rimmed sheet pan, and place chicken breast on the cooling rack.

3 Overnight

Place in the refrigerator, and allow to rest overnight to allow exterior of meat to dry out.

4 350°F (177°C)

Preheat the grill to 350°F (177°C) for indirect-heat cooking. Put the disposable aluminum roasting pan under the grate to catch dripping juices.

CHEF'S TIP

If you lift the grill lid before 20 minutes have passed, wait until the temperature inside the grill reaches 350°F (177°C) again before you start timing the cooking process again.

GRILL

Using tongs, place chicken breast side down on the grate over the drip pan. You may have to ball up a couple pieces of aluminum foil and place on either side to keep chicken straight. Place an in-oven meat thermometer in thickest part of thigh meat.

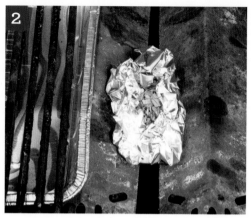

On a square of aluminum foil, place wood chips and roll up, leaving one end open. Put wrapped wood chips on the heat source.

Cover the grill, and smoke for 40 minutes, maintaining a temperature of 350°F (177°C). Turn chicken over.

20 minutes

Cover the grill again, return to 350°F (177°C), and smoke for 20 minutes, not opening the grill again until the thermometer reaches 155°F (68°C).

Remove chicken from the grill, place on a serving platter, and allow to rest for 15 minutes. The chicken will carryover cook to 165°F (74°C).

Remove the roasting pan from the grill. Strain, degrease, and taste accumulated juices or au jus, adjusting taste by adding kosher salt, black pepper, and chicken stock as needed. Serve chicken with au jus.

CHEF'S TIP

Allowing meat to sit in the refrigerator uncovered helps the exterior to dry out gives it a tacky feel, a process called *forming a pellicle*. When you smoke the meat now, you'll be smoking the dried-out meat instead of water that has accumulated on the exterior.

GRILL METHOD:
INDIRECT HEAT

PREP TIME:
10 MIN. + 12 HR.

COOK TIME:
2 HR.

SERVES: 6

Turkey Breast
with Salsa Verde

Most holidays, people find themselves around a table solidly weighed down with food, sometimes with a turkey as the centerpiece. The white meat cooks faster than the dark meat on a turkey, so when you cook a whole turkey, you end up with a dry breast before the dark meat is completely cooked. Because of both the amount of food and the problems with cooking a whole turkey, I instead like to cook a turkey breast at holidays. By cooking the turkey breast on the grill, you gain a little of the smoky qualities associated with the grill. When combined with a salsa verde, you bring a crispness to the dish that's cleansing to the palate.

INGREDIENTS

3 TB. kosher salt

1 TB. black pepper

1 TB. garlic salt

1 tsp. dried thyme

1 tsp. fresh rosemary, minced

½ tsp. celery salt

1 (6- to 7-lb. [2.75- to 3.25-lb.]) turkey breast, bone in

½ cup wood chips

2 cups chicken or turkey stock (optional)

2 cups Salsa Verde (see "Seasonings and Condiments")

TOOLS

Mixing bowl

Paper towels

Cooling rack

Sheet pan

Disposable aluminum roasting pan

Tongs

In-oven meat thermometer

Aluminum foil

Rimless cookie sheet

Cutting board

Sharp slicing knife

Serving platter

Meat fork

PREP

1

In a small mixing bowl, combine kosher salt, black pepper, garlic salt, thyme, rosemary, and celery salt, and mix well.

2

Dry turkey breast with paper towels, and rub seasoning mixture into all parts of meat.

3

Put a cooling rack on top of a sheet pan, and place turkey breast bone side down onto the cooling rack.

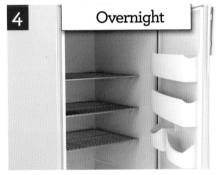

4 Overnight

Place in the refrigerator, and allow to rest overnight to allow exterior of skin to dry out.

GRILLING TRIVIA

The turkey was first bred in Mexico more than 2,000 years ago. Shortly after that, another breed was developed in the American Southwest; this breed is still commonly used in turkey dishes in that area.

GRILL

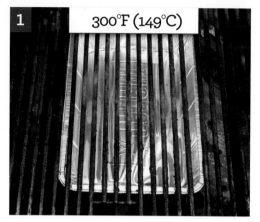

1   300°F (149°C)

Preheat the grill to 300°F (149°C) for indirect-heat cooking. Put a disposable aluminum roasting pan under the grate to catch dripping juices.

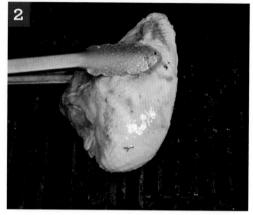

2

Using tongs, place turkey breast bone side down on the grate over the drip pan. Place an in-oven meat thermometer in thickest part of meat.

3

On a square of aluminum foil, place wood chips and roll up, leaving one end open. Put wrapped wood chips on the heat source.

4   2 hours

Cover the grill, and cook for 2 hours, maintaining a temperature of 300°F (149°C) and not opening the grill again until the thermometer reaches 155°F (68°C).

Slide turkey breast onto a rimless cookie sheet, move to a clean cutting board, and allow to rest for 15 minutes.

Remove the roasting pan from the grill. Strain, degrease, and taste accumulated juices or au jus, adjusting taste by adding kosher salt, black pepper, and chicken or turkey stock as needed.

Turkey should now be perfectly cooked. Remove breast from bone using a sharp slicing knife, and slice to your desired thickness across the grain. Place on a serving platter with a meat fork for pickup, and serve with Salsa Verde and au jus.

GRILL METHOD
INDIRECT HEAT

PREP TIME:
10 MIN. + 12 HR.

COOK TIME:
2–3 HR.

SERVES: 10

Whole Turkey
with Lemon-Coriander Rub

One doesn't automatically think of a grill when they talk turkey, but it's my preferred way of cooking the bird. I figured this out one year when we ran out of space in the oven during the holidays. Others wanted to put casseroles and potatoes in the oven at different temps, so the turkey made its way outdoors. I had to push snow off the top and take the warming rack off my grill, but the turkey turned out wonderfully. The breast was moist and the light smoke flavor was addictive. In this recipe, I add a coriander rub to perk up the turkey flavor.

INGREDIENTS

1 (10- to 12-lb. [4.5- to 5.5-kg]) whole turkey, thawed

1 cup Lemon-Coriander Rub (see "Seasonings and Condiments")

Pan spray

½ cup wood chips

2 cups chicken or turkey stock (optional)

TOOLS

Paper towels

Cooling rack

Sheet pan

Disposable aluminum roasting pan

Tongs

Aluminum foil

In-oven meat thermometer

Rimless cookie sheet

Cutting board

Sharp slicing knife

Serving platter

Meat fork

PREP

Dry turkey with paper towels, and spread Lemon-Coriander Rub into all parts of meat, including the cavity.

Put a cooling rack on top of a sheet pan, and place turkey breast side up onto the cooling rack.

Put in the refrigerator, and allow to rest overnight to allow exterior of skin to dry out.

Remove turkey from refrigerator, and spray outside with pan spray to put an oil coating on outside without losing rub in the process.

THAWING TURKEY

Don't forget to make sure your turkey is thawed before you cook it. The best way is to let it thaw in the refrigerator. This takes 1 day for every 4 pounds (1.75 kg) of turkey. So, for example, a 20-pound (9-kg) turkey will take 5 days to thaw. What if you don't have 5 days? Remove the wrapper from around the turkey, place it in the sink, and fill the sink with cold water. Every 30 minutes, drain the sink and refill it with new cold water. Allow 30 minutes per 1 pound (453.5 g) to defrost. For a 20-pound (9-kg) turkey, this means it'll take just 10 hours to defrost.

GRILL

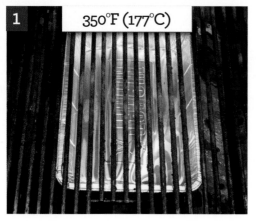

350°F (177°C)

Preheat the grill to 350°F (177°C) for indirect-heat cooking. Put a disposable aluminum roasting pan under the grate to catch dripping juices.

Using tongs, place turkey breast side down on the grate over the roasting pan. You may need to ball up a couple of pieces of aluminum foil to put under each side of turkey to keep it upright. Place an in-oven meat thermometer in thickest part of thigh meat.

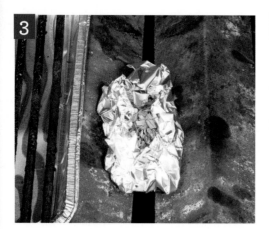

On a square of aluminum foil, place wood chips and roll up, leaving one end open. Put wrapped wood chips on the heat source.

1 hour + 30 min

Cover the grill, and cook for 1 hour and 30 minutes, maintaining a temperature of 350°F (177°C) and not opening the grill before then.

5

Turn turkey over, close the lid, and get the heat back up to 350°F (177°C) as quickly as possible. Cook until the thermometer reads 155°F (68°C), about 1 hour to 1 hour and 30 minutes.

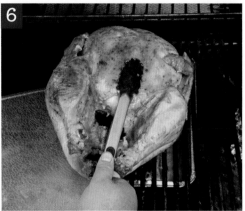

6

Slide turkey onto a rimless cookie sheet, move to a clean cutting board, and allow to rest on the cutting board for 20 minutes.

7

Remove the roasting pan from the grill. Strain, degrease, and taste the accumulated juices or au jus, adjusting the taste by adding kosher salt, black pepper, and chicken stock as needed.

8

Turkey should now be perfectly cooked. Carve with a sharp slicing knife, arrange on a serving platter with a meat fork for pickup, and serve with au jus.

CHEF'S TIP

Carving a whole turkey at the table is hard to do. I recommend removing each breast from the carcass, slicing it, and putting it on a platter. Next, remove the dark meat and arrange it on the outside of the platter. This may save you a trip to the emergency room when the turkey rolls off the platter as Grandpa is trying to cut it.

GRILL METHOD
DIRECT HEAT

PREP TIME:
5 MIN.

COOK TIME:
10 MIN.

SERVES: 4

Ground Turkey
with Peach Glaze

Ground turkey became very popular when people went on a search for low-fat alternatives to ground beef. True ground turkey can be a good substitute for ground beef, as long as you know what to look for. First of all, make sure that the processor hasn't added additional fats; many mixes have additional fat or oil so that it will brown as easily as beef. The marketing terms *lean* or *extra-lean* on the package can't be considered the only indicator. Second, make sure the processor hasn't added brine; this will keep the meat from browning until it is dried out. And don't be afraid of the grill heat here—you want high heat to brown the meat. These grilled turkey burgers are fabulous with the peach glaze, which really brings out the natural sweetness in the meat.

INGREDIENTS

2 lb. (907 g) ground turkey

2 TB. kosher salt

¼ TB. black pepper

¼ cup vegetable oil

1 cup Peach Glaze (see "Seasonings and Condiments")

4 hamburger buns

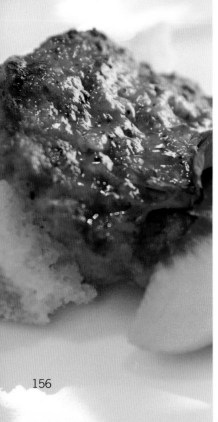

TOOLS

Mixing bowl

Transport tray

Tongs

Squirt bottle filled with water

Meat thermometer

Sauce mop

Serving platter

PREP

1 High

Preheat the grill to high for direct-heat cooking.

2

In a large mixing bowl, combine ground turkey, kosher salt, and black pepper. Form into 4 burgers the width of hamburger buns, and place on a transport tray. Rub both sides of turkey burgers with vegetable oil.

GRILL

1

Using tongs, place turkey burgers on the grill over direct heat, and allow to cook for 2 minutes. If flames start to burn up from the bottom of the grill, use the squirt bottle at the flame's base.

2

Rotate turkey burgers 45 degrees on the same side to make the cross-hatch pattern, and cook for 2 minutes. Flip, and repeat the same process on the other side.

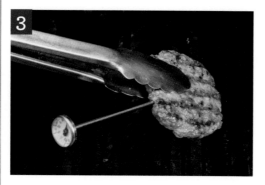

3

Put a meat thermometer through side of each turkey burger to check doneness, making sure at least 1 full inch (2.5 cm) of the thermometer stem is in meat. Turkey burgers should be cooked to 162°F (72°C).

4

Brush both sides with Peach Glaze using a sauce mop, and remove from the grill. Place on a serving platter, and allow to rest for 5 minutes to allow the juices to redistribute evenly. Serve.

157

GRILL METHOD
DIRECT HEAT

PREP TIME:
10 MIN.

COOK TIME:
12 MIN.

SERVES: 4

POULTRY

Duck Breasts
with Cherry Glaze

I love the flavor of duck. It's like a halfway point between chicken and pork and takes on the characteristics of a sauce so well. Yet people are scared to eat duck because they think it's greasy. However, the great thing about duck is that all its fat is on its outside, just under the skin; if the cook knows the right procedures for cooking, it should end up being lean in flavor. And by cooking it on the grill, you take it out of the rendered oils, making it less greasy. Plus, duck is more nutritious than other commercial meats. The cherry glaze added to it is a nod to tradition, when ducks were often raised on cherry orchards.

INGREDIENTS

4 duck breasts, skin on

3 TB. kosher salt

1 TB. black pepper

1 cup Cherry Glaze (see "Seasonings and Condiments")

TOOLS

Cutting boards

Paper towels

Sharp slicing knives

Cast-iron frying pan

Tongs

In-oven meat thermometer

Serving platter

PREP

On a cutting board, dry duck breasts with paper towels. Slice through skin just to meat on a diagonal every ½ inch (1.25 cm) using a sharp slicing knife.

Season duck breasts on both sides with kosher salt and black pepper.

Medium-High

Preheat the grill to medium-high for direct-heat cooking, placing the cast-iron frying pan on the grate over the hot part of the fire.

When the cast-iron pan is hot, put duck breasts in skin side down, and allow to cook until skin is golden brown and looks delicious, about 5 to 7 minutes.

CHEF'S TIP

Do *not* oil the exterior of duck as you would with most other grilled items. The oil will be rendered out of the skin side and will end up coating the duck in its natural oils.

POULTRY

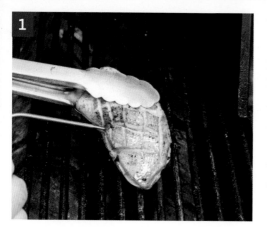

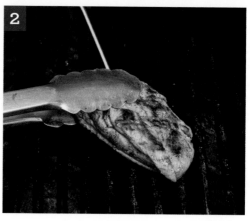

Remove duck breasts from the pan, turn over with tongs, and place meat side down on the hottest part of the grill. Place an in-oven probe thermometer in thickest part of a duck breast, and cook for 3 minutes.

Turn duck breasts 45 degrees to form the cross-hatch pattern, and cook for 3 minutes.

Turn over duck breasts to sautéed fat side to form the grill patterns, and cook until internal temperature has risen to 155°F (68°C), about 5 minutes. Remove from the grill, and place on a cutting board. Allow duck breasts to rest on the cutting board for 15 minutes. During this time, you'll notice that the internal temperature will climb to 165°F (74°C).

Drain oil from the frying pan, but leave all the flavor bits. Put Cherry Glaze into the pan to heat for 1 minute and absorb all those yummy bits left from sautéing.

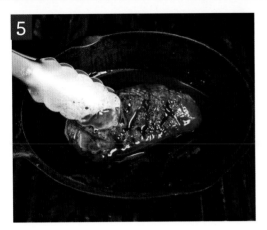

Dip cooked duck breasts in glaze. Place duck back on the cutting board, and slice on a bias using a sharp slicing knife. This allows you to make the muscle strands shorter and more tender and gives you 1½ servings from each breast.

Shingle duck slices on the serving platter, drizzle with a little additional glaze, and serve.

GRILL TRIVIA

There are three main varieties of duck. The most common is the Pekin. It's known for having a mild flavor and long breasts and is a descendant of the Mallard. Muscovy is a smaller bird with a darker, gamier flavor. Then there is the Mulard (not to be confused with Mallard), which is a genetic cross between the Pekin and Muscovy birds. Since the 1960s, this is the preferred bird for the production of foie gras in most of the world.

GRILL METHOD
INDIRECT HEAT

PREP TIME:
10 MIN. + 12 HR.

COOK TIME:
2 HR. + 10 MIN.

SERVES: 4

Whole Duck
with Allium Marinade

This duck recipe is time consuming, but the results are worth the wait. In the end, the skin is crispy and devoid of any of the oils, the meat is tender and juicy, and there's a wonderful tangy flavor that keeps you wanting to take another bite. The drip pan catches the oils, which make a great start for fried potatoes the next morning. My mouth is watering thinking about the flavor combination with the shallots in the marinade caramelizing and the rich, savory flavors of the duck.

INGREDIENTS

1 (4 ½- to 5-lb. [2- to 2.25-kg]) whole duck

2 cups Allium Marinade (see "Seasonings and Condiments")

1 cup chicken stock (optional)

TOOLS

Cutting boards

Sharp boning knives

Sauce brush

Sheet pan

Disposable aluminum roasting pan

Tongs

In-oven meat thermometer

Squirt bottle filled with water

Serving platter

PREP

On a cutting board, score a cross-hatch pattern across duck skin using a sharp boning knife; don't cut into meat.

Cut off flaps of fat at neck and body cavities.

Poke skin all over to create holes for hot oils to escape.

Brush inside and outside of duck with 1 cup Allium Marinade using a sauce brush. Place on a sheet pan, and put in the refrigerator to rest overnight.

Preheat the grill to 300°F (149°C) for indirect-heat cooking. Put a disposable aluminum roasting pan under the grate to catch dripping juices.

Using tongs, place duck breast side down on the grill over the roasting pan.

Cover the grill, and cook for 1 hour, maintaining a temperature of 300°F (149°C).

Turn over duck, and coat with ½ cup Allium Marinade.

Poke holes through skin again, put an in-oven meat thermometer in breast meat, and cook for 1 hour.

5

Brush duck with remaining ½ cup Allium Marinade. Move to the direct-heat side of the grill, putting breast side down, and cook 10 minutes to crisp skin. Squirt flames with water as needed using a squirt bottle.

6

Check to make sure internal temperature of duck is over 155°F (68°C). Remove from the grill, place on a clean cutting board, and allow to rest for 20 minutes.

7

Remove the drip pan from the grill. Strain, degrease, and taste pan juices or au jus, adjusting the taste by adding kosher salt, black pepper, and chicken stock as needed.

8

Remove breasts with a boning knife, and slice. Remove thigh meat. Shingle duck on a serving platter with thigh meat, and serve with au jus on the side.

FISH/
SEAFOOD

GRILL METHOD:
DIRECT HEAT

PREP TIME:
30 MIN.

COOK TIME:
15 MIN.

SERVES: 4

FISH/SEAFOOD

Salmon
with Orange-Ale Marinade

Salmon has gradually become so popular that you can find it in just about every restaurant today. While it's often a separate menu item, many places also offer it as an add-on item (for example, you can opt to add salmon to your Caesar salad or your pasta Alfredo). However, restaurants tend to overcook salmon to the point of being dry. This recipe shows you how to make a perfectly versatile grilled salmon. Orange and salmon are a great combination that brings together the bright fruit with the natural oils of the fish, so this recipe uses an orange-ale marinade.

INGREDIENTS

1 (1 ½- to 2 ¼-lb. [680.5-g to 1-kg]) piece salmon

1 cup Orange-Ale Marinade (see "Seasonings and Condiments")

3 TB. kosher salt

1 TB. black pepper

¼ cup vegetable oil

TOOLS

Paper towels

Cutting board

Chef's knife

Plastic zipper-lock bag

Tongs

Sauce brush

Offset spatula

Meat thermometer

Serving plates

PREP

1. Dry salmon with paper towels. With skin side on a cutting board, cut between skin and flesh to remove skin using a chef's knife. Once you start this process, you can grab salmon skin from under the knife and pull as you push the knife through; this should separate skin from flesh cleanly.

2. Clean the cutting board, chef's knife, and salmon of any scales, and then cut salmon into 4 pieces.

3. Put salmon in a plastic zipper-lock bag with ½ cup Orange-Ale Marinade, and squeeze out any air from the bag so salmon is completely covered by marinade. Place in the refrigerator, and allow to rest for a minimum of 20 minutes while you prep the grill.

High

4. Preheat the grill to high for direct-heat cooking.

5. Remove salmon from marinade, and pat dry with paper towels. Discard bag and used marinade.

6. Season salmon with kosher salt and black pepper, and coat with vegetable oil.

Using tongs, place salmon flesh side down on the grill over direct heat, and allow to cook for 2 minutes.

Rotate salmon 45 degrees to make the cross-hatch pattern, and cook for 2 minutes. If salmon sticks to the grill as you're trying to do this, just wait another minute before rotating. Flip salmon, and repeat the process on the other side.

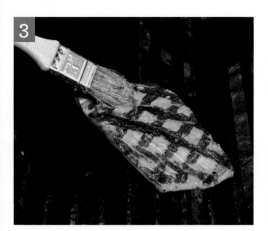

Move salmon to a cooler area of the grill, leaving skin side down, and brush top with remaining ½ cup Orange-Ale Marinade using a sauce brush.

Put a meat thermometer in salmon from the side to check doneness, making sure at least 1 full inch (2.5 cm) of the thermometer stem is in meat.

When salmon pieces reach an internal temperature of 140°F (60°C), remove from the grill using an offset spatula, and place on 4 serving plates.

Allow salmon to rest for 5 minutes; during this time, you'll notice the internal temperature continues to climb to 145°F (63°C). Center of salmon should still be opaque. Serve.

HOW LONG DOES IT TAKE SALMON TO COOK?

The time salmon takes to cook can vary widely based on the time of year the salmon was caught and the variety of salmon. Pacific salmon is pretty consistent, as they are fed a diet to help them grow fast in the farms. This diet often includes fats, such as beef suet or soy (high in fat), which help the fish to cook quickly.

Pacific Salmon has five primary species in North America and two in Asia. Two of the North American varieties (Chum and Sokeye) prefer to eat zooplankton their entire life. The other varieties (Chinook, Coho, Pink, Masa, and Amago) eat larger aquatic species as they get older, possibly including smelt, crab, shrimp, and krill. This diet of oily fish will increase the muscle fat (omega-3 fatty acids as well) in those salmon, and the higher fat content will make them cook much quicker than Chum or Sokeye.

GRILL METHOD
DIRECT HEAT

PREP TIME:
5 MIN.

COOK TIME:
10 MIN.

SERVES: 4

FISH/SEAFOOD

Tuna
with Thai Sauce

You can find tuna served many different ways, from raw in sashimi to well-done in tuna salad. It's recommended that fish be cooked to 145°F (63°C); however, if you want to serve the tuna at a lower temp, buy "sushi-grade" tuna. Sushi-grade tuna are actually flash-frozen to pasteurize them, which alleviates most of the foodborne illness concerns. In this recipe, you grill the tuna steaks to give them a little smoky character, and then add rich Asian flavors with a Thai sauce. The Thai sauce will meld together flavors of sweet tuna, rich grill and soy character, and bright ginger. This recipe is fabulous served with an udon noodle salad.

INGREDIENTS

4 (5- to 6-oz. [141.75- to 170-g]) tuna steaks

2 TB. kosher salt

¼ TB. black pepper

¼ cup vegetable oil

1 cup Thai Sauce (see "Seasonings and Condiments")

TOOLS

Paper towels

Transport tray

Offset spatula

Squirt bottle filled with water

Serving plates

PREP

Dry tuna steaks with paper towels. Season with kosher salt and black pepper, coat with vegetable oil, and place on a transport tray.

High

Preheat the grill to high for direct-heat cooking.

GRILL

Using an offset spatula, place tuna steaks on the grill over direct heat, and allow to cook for 1 minute.

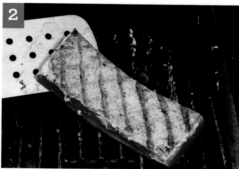

Rotate tuna steaks 45 degrees, and cook for 1 minute. If they stick as you're trying to do this, just wait another minute before rotating. Flip tuna steaks, and repeat the process on the other side.

Move tuna steaks to a cooler area of the grill, and put a thermometer in the middle of each. When tuna steaks reach an internal temperature of 120°F (49°C), remove from the grill, and place on serving plates.

Allow tuna steaks to rest for 5 minutes. Serve with Thai Sauce.

GRILL METHOD
INDIRECT HEAT

PREP TIME:
5 MIN.

COOK TIME:
12 MIN.

SERVES: 4

FISH/SEAFOOD

Halibut
with Pesto

Halibut falls into the white-fleshed-fish category of lean fish, meaning it's not as firm, cooks more slowly, and is less forgiving. No worries; this recipe is foolproof. Instead of direct heat, you will use indirect—that way, you won't have to move it as much and will be able to watch the temperature more closely. I like to substitute hazelnuts instead of pine nuts in the pesto, because they pair with this fish better.

INGREDIENTS

4 (6- to 7-oz. [170- to 198.5-g]) halibut steaks

2 TB. sea salt

1 tsp. ground white pepper

¼ cup vegetable oil

½ cup wood chips

2 cups Pesto (see "Seasonings and Condiments")

TOOLS

Paper towels

Sheet pan

Disposable aluminum roasting pan

Offset spatula

In-oven meat thermometer

Aluminum foil

Serving platter

Dry halibut steaks with paper towels. Season all sides with kosher salt and white pepper. Place halibut steaks on a sheet pan, and return to refrigerator, uncovered, while you prepare the grill.

400°F (204°C)

Preheat the grill to 400°F (204°C) for indirect-heat cooking. Put a disposable aluminum roasting pan under the grate.

Using an offset spatula, place halibut steaks on the grate over the roasting pan. Place an in-oven meat thermometer in center of largest piece of halibut.

On a square of aluminum foil, place wood chips and roll up, leaving one end open. Put wrapped wood chips on the heat source.

12 minutes

Cover the grill, and cook for about 12 minutes, maintaining a temperature of 400°F (204°C) and not opening the grill until halibut reaches an internal temperature of 140°F (60°C).

Remove halibut steaks from the grill, and place on a serving platter. Coat each with ¼ cup Pesto, and serve with remaining 1 cup Pesto on the platter.

GRILL METHOD
DIRECT HEAT

PREP TIME:
5 MIN.

COOK TIME:
8 MIN.

SERVES: 4

FISH/ SEAFOOD

Grouper
with Cajun Rub

Grouper is a marine water fish that has firm flesh, especially for a member of the white-flesh family. The flavor is mild and sweet, so you have to pay attention to how you pair it with sauces and seasoning—add too many, and you won't be able to taste the fish. This recipe pairs it with a Cajun rub. The rub is slightly spicy and sweet, so keep it to the amount called for; if you put too much, you'll end up just tasting the heat of the rub. Also, look for four pieces similar in width, so they'll all cook at about the same rate.

INGREDIENTS

4 (6- to 7-oz. [170- to 198.5-g]) grouper filets

½ cup Cajun Rub (see "Seasonings and Condiments")

2 TB. vegetable oil

TOOLS

Paper towels

Transport tray

Offset spatula

Meat thermometer

Serving plates

PREP

1

Dry grouper filets with paper towels. Season with Cajun Rub, coat with vegetable oil, and place on a transport tray.

2 High

Preheat the grill to high for direct-heat cooking.

GRILL

1

Using an offset spatula, place grouper filets on the grill over direct heat, and allow to cook for 2 minutes.

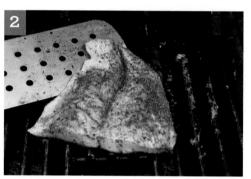

2

Rotate grouper filets 45 degrees, and cook for 2 minutes. If they stick as you're trying to do this, just wait another minute before rotating. Flip grouper filets, and repeat the process on the other side.

3

Move grouper filets to a cooler area of the grill, and put a meat thermometer in middle of one to check doneness. When grouper reaches an internal temperature of 140°F (60°C), remove from the grill, and place on serving plates.

4

Allow grouper filets to rest for 5 minutes. Serve.

177

GRILL METHOD:
DIRECT HEAT

PREP TIME:
5 MIN.

COOK TIME:
4 MIN.

SERVES: 4

Scallops
with Watermelon-Jicama Salsa

Scallops are fantastic when grilled to a nice, crisp crust with an opaque middle. For optimal grilling, it's imperative that you use dry-pack scallops, as normal scallops are packed in a chemical that helps them stay plump over time but also makes it difficult to brown them. The flavor of scallops is so delicate and sweet, this is another seafood to which the "less is more" rule applies. The more you season it or put it in rich sauces, the less flavor you get from the scallops. Therefore, this recipe uses a mild watermelon-jicama salsa for flavor.

INGREDIENTS

12 U-10-size scallops

1 TB. sea salt

2 TB. vegetable oil

1 cup Watermelon-Jicama Salsa (see "Seasonings and Condiments")

TOOLS

Paper towels

Transport tray

Tongs

Serving plates

PREP

1

Dry scallops with paper towels. Season with sea salt, coat with vegetable oil, and place on a transport tray.

2 High

Preheat the grill to high for the direct-heat cooking.

GRILL

1

Using tongs, place scallops on the grate of the grill over direct heat, and allow to cook for 1 minute.

2

Rotate scallops 45 degrees, and cook for 1 minute. If they stick as you're trying to do this, just wait another minute before rotating. Flip scallops, and repeat the process on the other side.

3

Move scallops to a cooler area of the grill, and put a thermometer in middle of each to check the doneness. When scallops reach an internal temperature of 140°F (60°C), remove from the grill, and place on serving plates. Allow to rest for 5 minutes. Serve with Watermelon-Jicama Salsa.

GRILLING TRIVIA

When buying scallops and shrimp, the number listed for sizing refers to how many of them it takes to add up to 1 pound (453.5 g). Thus, with 28–32 size shrimp, there are 28 to 32 in a pound. They are often sold in 3-pound (1.5-kg) boxes, so when you multiply the number by the average, you can come up with the number of pieces in the box. The largest of the sizes is normally U-10 (under 10 in a pound).

GRILL METHOD:
DIRECT HEAT

PREP TIME:
40 MIN.

COOK TIME:
3 MIN.

SERVES: 10

FISH/
SEAFOOD

Shrimp
with Cocunut Marinade

There are many different options when buying shrimp. If you're going to cook it, buy the raw shrimp rather than the cooked. This recipe uses shrimp with the shell on, but if you don't like peeling shrimp, buy it peeled already. If the shrimp is going to stand alone on the plate, look for a bigger size, which means a lower size number. If you get below a size 21, you will need to skewer them together to keep them from falling through the grate and into the coals. And for a familiar flavor pairing, this recipe uses a coconut marinade with the shrimp.

INGREDIENTS

3 lb. (1.5-kg) 21–25-size raw shrimp, shell on

1 cup Coconut Marinade (see "Seasonings and Condiments")

TOOLS

Tongs

Cutting board

Paring knives

Plastic zipper-lock bag

Serving platter

PREP

If you're buying peeled and deveined shrimp, skip to Prep 5.

Preheat the grill to high for direct-heat cooking.

If you bought shell-on shrimp, using tongs, place shrimp on the grill, and cook for 30 seconds. Flip over, and cook for 30 seconds. Remove shrimp from the grill, and place in the refrigerator to cool for 10 minutes.

Remove shrimp from the refrigerator, and place on a cutting board. Starting at the legs, grip edge of shell and pull around; the layers of shell should come off fairly easily. Unless you're going to serve tail as a finger food, pull off tail.

Run a paring knife along back of shrimp, just cutting surface. Remove black line that runs just under surface. If you don't see one, don't worry; most of the time, farmers purge shrimp so there isn't anything left there.

Put shrimp into a plastic zipper-lock bag with ½ cup Coconut Marinade, and squeeze out any air in the bag so shrimp is completely covered by marinade. Place in the refrigerator, and allow to marinate for 20 minutes.

Remove shrimp from marinade, and shake off any excess. Discard bag and marinade.

GRILL

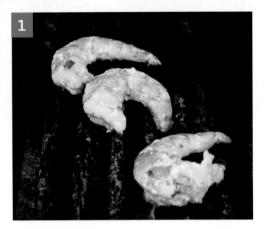

Place shrimp on the grill over direct heat, and allow to cook for 1 minute.

Flip shrimp, and cook for 1 minute.

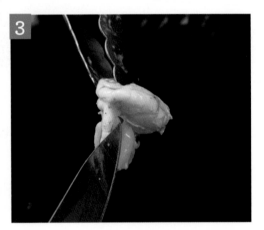

Cut into one of shrimp with a paring knife to see if middle has turned an opaque white. If not, give shrimp another minute.

Remove from the grill, place on a serving platter, and serve with remaining ½ cup Coconut Marinade.

WHY COOK THE SHRIMP WITH THE SHELL ON?

Much of the flavor of shrimp is in the shell itself. By giving it a quick cook with the shell on, you push some of those flavors into the shrimp meat and therefore end up with a much better shrimp flavor.

CHEF'S TIP

Know where your shrimp comes from. A majority of shrimp comes from fish farms. Because of the preferred growing environment, the shrimp are often farmed in estuaries; these farms can totally kill the estuaries were they are placed because of how much they throw off the delicate ecosystem. If they are wild caught, they're often caught by dragging nets on the bottom, which ends up with a large amount of by-catch and ruins any coral growth on the bottom.

There are some great resources to find out what are good seafood to buy and which you should stay clear of. The Monterey Bay Aquarium, Fishline, and the World Wildlife Federation all keep downloadable lists of what is good and what is bad.

GRILL METHOD:
DIRECT HEAT

PREP TIME:
20 MIN.

COOK TIME:
4 MIN.

SERVES: 4

FISH/SEAFOOD

Shrimp Cowboy
with Memphis Barbecue Sauce

Bacon and shrimp together—what's not to love? This recipe is a great variation on plain shrimp; they make great hors d'oeuvres that are true crowd pleasers. My favorite way to serve them is as a topping on a thick steak. The bacon and barbecue sauce–coated shrimp have a meaty quality that goes well with the beef or can make them stand on their own as an hors d'oeuvre. I prefer to use wild-caught Key West Pink shrimp for this recipe, as they have a more intense, sweet flavor. It's definitely worth spending a couple extra dollars for them.

INGREDIENTS

1 lb. (453.5 g) 21–25-size raw shrimp, shell on

1 lb. (453.5 g) bacon

1 TB. sea salt

1 tsp. black pepper

½ cup Memphis Barbecue Sauce (see "Seasonings and Condiments")

TOOLS

Wooden toothpicks

Cutting board

Paring knives

Chef's knife

Sheet pan

Tongs

Serving platter

PREP

If you're buying peeled and deveined shrimp, skip to Prep 5.

Preheat the grill to high for direct-heat cooking.

Soak 25 wooden toothpicks in water. Preheat the oven to 400°F (204°C).

On a cutting board, place shrimp, and starting at the legs, grip edge of shell and pull around; the layers of shell should come off fairly easily. Unless you're going to serve as a finger food, pull off tail.

Run a paring knife along back of shrimp, just cutting surface. Remove black line that runs just under surface. If you don't see one, don't worry; most of the time, farmers purge shrimp so there isn't anything left there.

Cut bacon strips in half with a chef's knife, and lay out on a sheet pan. Bake in a 400°F (204°C) oven for about 10 minutes to cook about halfway.

Season shrimp with sea salt and black pepper, and wrap each shrimp with 1 piece bacon. Put wooden toothpick through each to hold bacon in place.

185

GRILL

Using tongs, place shrimp on the grill over direct heat, and allow to cook for 2 minutes.

Flip over shrimp, and cook for 2 minutes.

Cut into middle of one of shrimp with a paring knife to see if middle has turned white. If not, cook another minute.

Dip each shrimp in Memphis Barbecue Sauce, lay out on a serving platter, and serve.

RECIPE VARIATIONS

Want to expand on this recipe? You can wrap the shrimp in different things to develop different flavors and pair with certain dishes.

Wrap With	Flavor/Texture	Serve With
Bacon	Smoky and salty	Steak
Ham	Sweet and salty	Pork
Wonton	Crunchy	Rice
Green onion stems	Fresh and summery	Seafood

GRILLING TRIVIA

Shrimp are synonymous with prawns, and the names are interchanged in different areas. They are found in the sea, estuaries, lakes, and rivers of the world. There are thousands of varieties, each adapting to their own environment. The commercial shrimp business was $50 billion (36,840,567,002 euros) in 2010, making shrimp the number-one seafood in the world.

GRILL METHOD
INDIRECT HEAT

PREP TIME:
10 MIN.

COOK TIME:
5-10 MIN.

SERVES: 4

FISH/SEAFOOD

Lobster Tails

Lobster is a crustacean that cooks very quickly; this recipe shows how to cook the tail. Lobster tails are usually found in the freezer section of the grocery store. If you don't have a good pair of kitchen shears, look for tails that have already been split. If your store does have fresh lobster, you can ask the butcher to separate the tail for you. Don't forget to have some melted butter ready for your guests to dip this succulent meat into.

CHEF'S TIP

Lobster tail is an excellent accompaniment to a grilled steak to make it a classic "surf and turf" combination.

INGREDIENTS

4 lobster tails

1 TB. kosher salt

1 tsp. black pepper

1 cup melted butter

½ cup wood chips

TOOLS

Disposable aluminum roasting pan

Cutting board

Kitchen shears

Sauce brush

Transport tray

Tongs

Aluminum foil

Serving platter

PREP

1 400°F (204°C)

Preheat the grill to 400°F (204°C) for indirect-heat cooking. Put a disposable aluminum roasting pan under the grate to catch dripping juices.

2

On a cutting board, in center of top of each lobster tail shell, use kitchen shears to cut down to last segment of tail. You want the blade just under shell, but not in meat.

3

Turn tails over, and cut down middle of underside for each, making sure to cut shell but not into meat.

4

Pull two halves of the shell apart for each, being careful not to tear them completely apart. You want last segment to stay hinged together.

5

Pull lobster meat out until you get to the point where meat is still attached to tail end. Lay lobster meat across top of shell for each, and put shell back together underneath.

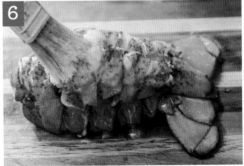

6

Season lobster meat with kosher salt and black pepper, brush with ¼ cup melted butter using a sauce brush, and place on a transport tray.

GRILL

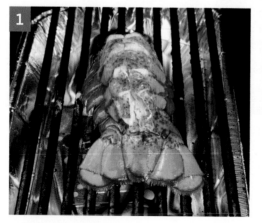

Using tongs, put lobster tails on the grill over the roasting pan, spacing them out so there's plenty of airflow between each.

On a square of aluminum foil, place wood chips and roll up, leaving one end open. Put wrapped wood chips on the heat source.

Cover the grill. When the temperature inside the grill has recovered to 400°F (204°C), cook for 5 minutes.

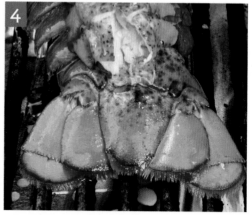

Check lobster tails for doneness; lobster shells should be red and meat should be milky white all the way across. If this isn't the case, close the grill lid, and cook for 5 minutes.

FISH/SEAFOOD

Remove lobster tails from the grill, and brush meat with ¼ cup melted butter.

Put lobster tails on a serving platter, and serve with remaining ½ cup melted butter.

GRILLING TRIVIA

Lobster is considered a luxury food today, but it has humble beginnings. Lobsters were so thick on the shorelines when European settlers came to the United States, they reported piles 4 feet (1.25 m) tall would wash ashore. It became a food that was served to prisoners and servants because it was so cheap and plentiful. In the nineteenth century, special lobster boats were invented to keep lobsters alive when caught, which is what helped change the thinking on them to be more of a luxury food.

GRILL METHOD:
INDIRECT HEAT

PREP TIME:
20 MIN.

COOK TIME:
5-10 MIN.

SERVES: 4

Lobster
with Garlic-Herb Compound Butter

The smells that develop while this recipe is cooking will bring the neighborhood to your backyard. This recipe takes the meat from the lobster, mixes it with herb-rich whole butter, and puts it back into the body of the lobster. So as it finally cooks, each bite-size piece of meat is dripping with buttery goodness.

INGREDIENTS

4 (2- to 4-lb. [907-g to 1.75-kg]) lobsters

2 lb. (907-g) Garlic-Herb Compound Butter

TOOLS

Cutting board

Chef's knife

Kitchen shears

Mixing bowl

Disposable aluminum roasting pan

Tongs

Serving platter

PREP

Put lobsters on a cutting board. For each, place a chef's knife at top of head between eyes, and cut straight down and forward between eyes, killing it.

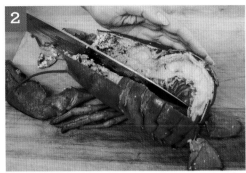

Cut lobster back the other direction so each is cut in half lengthwise.

Pull off claw arms of each lobster.

Using the side of a food mallet, crack open claws, and remove meat; set claws aside. Pick over meat to make certain you've removed all shell pieces.

On main body halves, remove tail meat and set aside. Remove remaining parts from inside the lobster body, and rinse the cavity out.

Cut lobster meat into bite-size pieces, and place in a medium mixing bowl. Add Garlic-Herb Compound Butter, and gently fold lobster pieces into butter.

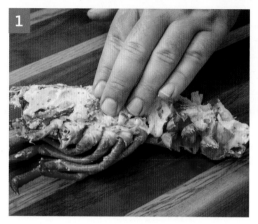

Using half lobster bodies like bowls, put lobster meat-compound butter mixture into shells.

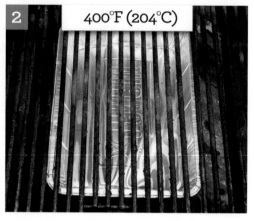

Preheat the grill to 400°F (204°C) for indirect-heat cooking. Put a disposable aluminum roasting pan under the grate to catch dripping juices.

Using tongs, put lobsters on the grill shell side down over the roasting pan, spacing them out so there's plenty of airflow between each.

Cover the grill. When the temperature inside the grill has recovered to 400°F (204°C), cook for 5 minutes.

Check lobsters for doneness; lobster shells should be red, meat should be milky white, and butter should be melted. If this isn't the case, close the grill, and cook for 5 more minutes.

Remove lobsters from the grill, put on a serving platter, and serve.

HANDLING LOBSTER

If you don't feel comfortable cutting up the live lobster, you can blanch it in boiling water. Bring a pot of water big enough to hold the lobster to a boil. Next, place the lobster headfirst into the pot, and allow it to boil for 3 minutes. This will kill the lobster and make it a little easier to work with.

GRILL METHOD:
INDIRECT HEAT

PREP TIME:
20 MIN.+ 1 HR.

COOK TIME:
6 MIN.

SERVES: 4

Crab Cakes
with Papaya-Mint Salsa

Crab cakes are a true American classic. This dish first appeared in writings by colonists as a minced crab pie, and it wasn't until 1930 that the term "crab cake" was used. The blue crabs from the Chesapeake Bay area are said to be the best for crab cakes, but almost any type of crab can be used. The crab cakes have a rich flavor accented with the smoky flavors of bacon and the hint of celery salt from Old Bay seasoning.

INGREDIENTS

Zest of 2 limes

1 green onion, white and green parts, chopped

3 oz. (85 g) cooked bacon, chopped

6 TB. mayonnaise

1 large egg

5 TB. breadcrumbs

2 tsp. Old Bay seasoning

1 ½ tsp. sea salt

1 ½ lb. (680.5 g) lump crab meat

Pan spray

1 cup Papaya-Mint Salsa (see "Seasonings and Condiments")

TOOLS

Mixing bowl

Sheet pan

Offset spatula

Serving platter

PREP

In a medium mixing bowl, combine lime zest, green onion, cooked bacon, mayonnaise, egg, breadcrumbs, Old Bay seasoning, and sea salt. Mix to combine well, but not so much that mixture becomes a wet, soggy mess.

Pick through crab meat to check for pieces of shell.

Add crab to mixing bowl, and combine. This should be a loose mixture; don't overwork.

Make crab mixture into patties lightly; don't overpack crab cakes.

Lay crab cakes on a sheet pan, and spray both sides with pan spray.

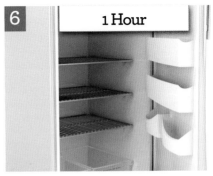

Put crab cakes in the refrigerator for a minimum of 1 hour to allow starches and proteins to come together and form a more solid patty.

GRILL

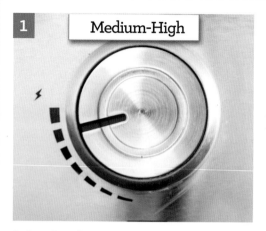

Medium-High

Preheat the grill to medium-high for direct-heat cooking.

Using an offset spatula, place crab cakes on the grill over direct heat, and cook for 2 minutes.

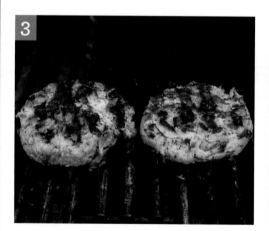

Carefully turn over crab cakes, and cook for 2 minutes. Because of the delicate nature of crab cakes, you may not want to try to form the cross-hatch pattern on them.

Put a thermometer in side of a crab cake to check for doneness. Crab cake is done when it reaches an internal temperature of 155°F (68°C).

5

Remove crab cakes from the grill, place on a serving platter, and serve garnished with Papaya-Mint Salsa.

CHEF'S TIP

These crab cakes are rarely served alone. They can be served on a sandwich with a creamy mayonnaise-based sauce or on a salad with mixed greens. Or you can even find them at sporting events served with "crab fries"—french fries seasoned heavily with Old Bay seasoning. Personally, I like to eat them on a salad of Arugula greens and roasted red peppers.

GRILL METHOD:
DIRECT HEAT

PREP TIME:
20 MIN.

COOK TIME:
6 MIN.

SERVES: 4

Oysters
with Garlic-Herb Compound Butter

Oysters are a wonderful meal, as long as you can get them when they're really fresh. They have a delicate sweet-and-brine balance that makes your mouth want more. This recipe heats the shelled oysters directly over the grill to melt the herb butter. In an ideal world, as you eat the oyster, you'll feel the warm butter followed by the cool oyster. It's a treat for all of your senses.

INGREDIENTS

16 fresh oysters

1 cup Garlic-Herb Compound Butter
   (see "Seasonings and Condiments")

TOOLS

Kitchen towel

Oyster knife

Transport tray

Tongs

Serving platter

PREP

For each oyster, look at both shells on oyster—one is pretty flat, while the other is more rounded. Leave rounded side down so liquid stays in as you open oyster.

Roll up a kitchen towel, leaving out a flap of about 2 inches (5 cm). Place rounded end of oyster in the towel where the roll meets the flap. This should leave the part of the oyster that has a hinge sticking out of the back.

Put one hand behind the towel roll to hold oyster. This way, if the oyster knife slips out of oyster as you're shucking, it should go into the towel and not your hand.

With the oyster knife in your other hand, put point between hinge and pry open.

Run the knife around inside tip of oyster to free meat from shell. Repeat on bottom shell, being careful to leave as much juice as you can in shell.

Discard top shell, and line up bottom shells with meat on a transport tray.

GRILL

1 Medium-High

Preheat the grill to medium-high for direct-heat cooking.

2 Put 1 tablespoon Garlic-Herb Compound Butter on top of each oyster.

3 Using tongs, place oysters on the grill over direct heat, and cook for 6 minutes. You may have to slide shells a bit to keep them balanced upright.

4 Once butter is melted, remove oysters from the grill, place on a serving platter, and serve.

CHEF'S TIP

Starting a dinner with champagne is a great way to set the tone of the meal. Oysters and champagne are the perfect paring together. Champagne has a naturally high acid level, while oysters have a high salt content; when combined together, they balance each other out. Serving this dish is a great way to start a dinner party, with guests enjoying oysters and champagne. And as guests arrive, you don't have to worry about food getting cold—the shells will stay warm for a long time.

FLAVORS OF OYSTERS

From	Flavor
Tasmania, Australia	Creamy and slightly sweet with a crisp finish
Namibian, Nambia	Plump with mineral flavors of copper, zinc, and steel
Santa Catrina, Brazil	Salty and vegetal
Kelly Galway, Ireland	Large with a soy sauce-like flavor
Speciales Gillardeau, France	Tender with a miso broth-like flavor
Senpoushi, Japan	Delicate with a soft saltiness
Hog Island, United States	Sweet with pleasant brine flavors

GRILL METHOD:
DIRECT HEAT

PREP TIME:
5 MIN.

COOK TIME:
10-12 MIN.

SERVES: 4

FISH/SEAFOOD

Clams

Clams may be the easiest things to cook on the grill—it's just a matter of cleaning and tossing them on to warm. Yet the simplicity brings out the true flavor of this shellfish and makes it seem magical. All the shells lined up on the grill, seemingly void of anything happening, then—pop, pop, pop— they start to open, and the hidden flesh now visible, with the natural juices cupped in the bottom of the shell.

RECIPE VARIATION

You don't have to be limited to clams. Mussels can also be used interchangeably in this recipe.

INGREDIENTS

2 lb. (907 g) clams

1 lemon, cut into ⅓-in. (1-cm) slices

1 TB. vegetable oil

1 sprig rosemary

½ cup melted butter

TOOLS

Transport tray

Tongs

Serving bowl

PREP

Medium

Preheat the grill to medium for direct-heat cooking. Go through clams and discard any that don't close when given a little tap or are visibly cracked or broken.

Scrub outsides of shells under running water to get any dirt off, pull off beards (the seaweed-looking stuff hanging from corner of shells), and place on a transport tray. Coat lemon slices with vegetable oil.

GRILL

Using tongs, put clams in a single layer on the grill over direct heat. Put lemon slices on the grill, and lay rosemary sprig on top of clams.

As clams begin to open, after 10 to 12 minutes, put them into a serving bowl. Be careful not to turn upside-down so that juice doesn't run out. Place lemons in the bowl after they have light grill marks on them.

Pour melted butter over clams, put sprig of rosemary on top to add aroma, and serve.

GRILL METHOD:
INDIRECT HEAT

PREP TIME:
10 MIN.

COOK TIME:
1 HR.

SERVES: 4

Artichokes
Italian Stuffed

Commonly in Italy, people serve a grilled artichoke in the middle of the table, with everyone pulling leaves and eating off one artichoke. This recipe shows you how to enjoy this great delicacy without the troubles associated with cooking artichokes, such as getting stuck by the little points or not being able to cut out the fuzzy choke. Once you're done and you begin pulling off each leaf and scraping the little meat into your mouth, you'll know it was worth the time to cook it. And when you cut into the bottom and bite into the meat, you'll wish you had more.

INGREDIENTS

2 artichokes

2 lemons, cut in half

1 cup seasoned breadcrumbs

¼ cup fresh basil, chopped

1 TB. fresh oregano, chopped

¼ cup sun-dried tomatoes, chopped

1 cup Parmesan cheese, shredded

4 cloves garlic, minced

1 egg

¼ cup chicken broth

2 TB. extra-virgin olive oil

TOOLS

Cutting board

Chef's knife

Kitchen scissors

Melon baller

Disposable aluminum roasting pan

Mixing bowl

Toothpicks

Aluminum foil

Tongs

Serving platter

PREP

1 Wash artichokes in cold water, pulling on each leaf and opening a little to allow water to run through each petal. Pour oil over the lemon halves.

2 On a cutting board, cut bottom stem end of each artichoke so they sit flat using a chef's knife. Immediately rub cut ends with lemon pulp (the juicy inner flesh) to keep them from oxidizing (turning brown).

3 Cut point off each artichoke leaf using kitchen scissors, making sure to throw points away. Cut artichokes in half lengthwise, and immediately rub lemon pulp on each exposed half.

4 Scoop out fuzzy choke in the center of each using a melon baller. Rinse insides to get out any remaining choke, and immediately squeeze lemon juice into exposed areas.

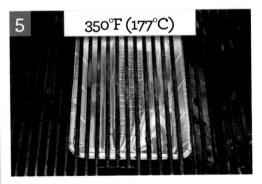

350°F (177°C)

5 Preheat the grill to 350°F (177°C) for indirect-heat cooking. Put a disposable aluminum roasting pan under the grate.

6 In a medium mixing bowl, combine seasoned breadcrumbs, basil, oregano, sun-dried tomatoes, Parmesan cheese, and garlic.

Add egg, chicken broth, and extra-virgin olive oil, and mix.

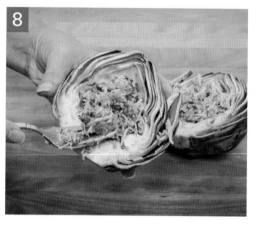

Put stuffing mixture in the center of artichokes.

Put two halves of each artichoke back together, and put a toothpick through each side to secure.

Pull each leaf outward, and put half of stuffing mixture in each. Wrap artichokes upright in aluminum foil.

GRILL

Using tongs, place wrapped artichokes on the grill over indirect heat, and allow to cook for 50 minutes.

Remove artichokes from the foil, and cook for 10 minutes to allow stuffing to brown.

Remove artichokes from the grill, arrange on a serving platter, and serve.

GRILLING TRIVIA

Artichokes are part of the thistle family. They're a flower bud that, if allowed to grow, would be a spectacular purple bloom. The best time to get artichokes is March to May, when they're in peak production. Look for artichokes that are green with very little browning. The leaves should be tight to the center, not curling outward.

GRILL METHOD:
DIRECT HEAT

PREP TIME:
10 MIN.

COOK TIME:
4-6 MIN.

SERVES: 4

VEGETABLES

Asparagus
with Allium Marinade

Asparagus is one of my favorite things to grill. For me, when the asparagus starts to come in, it's a sign that spring is officially here. This is the first of the spring veggies and starts a long line of vegetables that will hit the grill over the next several months. As you work with asparagus, separate the spears so they're grouped by how thick they are; the time it takes to cook will vary by this thickness. Be mindful that the tips of the asparagus are tender and should be treated with care.

CHEF'S TIP

Putting the asparagus spears on skewers helps with turning and keeps you from losing a stray spear though the grill grate.

INGREDIENTS

20 asparagus spears

1 cup Allium Marinade (see "Seasonings and Condiments")

TOOLS

Bamboo skewers soaked in water

Sauce brush

Tongs

Serving platter

PREP

Preheat the grill to high for direct-heat cooking.

Rinse asparagus spears thoroughly, and snap off tough, woody ends.

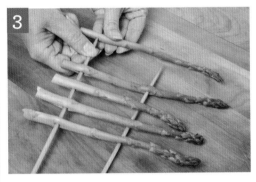

Line up 5 spears next to each other, and push a wet bamboo skewer through them about ½ inch (1.25 cm) below tips. Push a second wet bamboo skewer the same distance from the base. Repeat for remaining spears.

Brush spears with ½ cup Allium Marinade using a sauce brush.

GRILL

Using tongs, place asparagus skewers on the grill over direct heat, and cook for about 2 minutes. Remove from the grill, and brush with remaining ½ cup Allium Marinade.

Return to the grill on the other side, and cook until cooked through, about 2 more minutes. Remove asparagus spears from the skewers, arrange on a serving platter, and serve.

GRILL METHOD:
INDIRECT HEAT

PREP TIME:
10 MIN.

COOK TIME:
30 MIN.

SERVES: 6

Cabbage

When cabbage is cooked right, it has a wonderful flavor and texture. Unfortunately, it has gotten a bad rap because of all the people who let it cook all day. The longer it cooks, the more a chemical reaction happens that causes it to release a foul odor. In this recipe, you only need to cook it until it starts to soften. A little bacon in the mix will also draw more appreciation from your family and guests—meanwhile, the high vitamin and mineral content in cabbage will round out a healthy meal.

INGREDIENTS

1 head green cabbage

6 TB. butter

3 tsp. kosher salt

3 tsp. ground black pepper

6 TB. Parmesan cheese, shredded

6 slices bacon

TOOLS

Disposable aluminum roasting pan

Cutting board

Chef's knife

Aluminum foil

Tongs

Serving platter

214

PREP

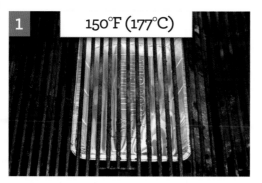

150°F (177°C)

Preheat the grill to 350°F (177°C) for indirect-heat cooking. Put a disposable aluminum roasting pan under the grate.

On a cutting board, cut green cabbage into 6 wedges using a chef's knife, and place each wedge on a square of aluminum foil.

Top each cabbage wedge with butter, kosher salt, black pepper, Parmesan cheese, and 1 slice bacon.

Seal cabbage wedges in the aluminum foil.

GRILL

Using tongs, put wrapped cabbage wedges on the grill, and cook for 30 minutes.

Remove cabbage wedges from the grill, and open the foil carefully, as steam will come out when opened. Arrange cabbage wedges on a serving platter, and serve.

GRILL METHOD:
DIRECT HEAT

PREP TIME:
10 MIN.

COOK TIME:
10 MIN.

SERVES: 4

VEGETABLES

Carrots
with Lemon-Coriander Rub

This recipe is best when you can get good, locally grown carrots. The fresher the carrots are, the more sugars and water they'll contain. This will combine when cooked to produce nice caramelization on the outside of the carrots and a soft, creamy interior. The lemon-coriander rub adds a rich, meaty character to the end of the flavor palate.

CHEF'S TIP

There are many varieties of carrots that come in red, purple, orange, and white. Serving carrots in range of colors can create interest on the plate. This also helps you provide a larger variety of nutrients in your diet, because each type has a different combination of vitamins and minerals.

If you can, find carrots at a farmer's market, or better yet, grow your own. Look for carrots that have been through at least one hard frost, as the freeze causes the carrot to start to produce even more sugars.

INGREDIENTS

1 lb. (453.5 g) whole carrots

3 TB. Lemon-Coriander Rub (see "Seasonings and Condiments")

2 TB. butter, melted

TOOLS

Cutting board
Peeler
Chef's knife
Transport tray

Tongs
Meat fork
Serving platter

PREP

Medium-High

Preheat the grill to medium-high for direct-heat cooking.

On a cutting board, peel carrots using a peeler, cut in half lengthwise using a chef's knife, and rub liberally with Lemon-Coriander Rub. Place carrots on a transport tray to take to the grill.

GRILL

Place carrots on the grill curved side down over direct heat, and allow to cook for 5 minutes.

Turn over carrots with tongs, and cook until soft all the way through, about 5 more minutes. To check doneness, poke carrot with a meat fork. If carrot sticks to the fork, it's not ready; if carrot falls off the fork, it's ready.

Remove carrots from the grill, place on a serving platter, brush with melted butter, and serve.

GRILL METHOD:
DIRECT HEAT

PREP TIME:
20 MIN.

COOK TIME:
15 MIN.

SERVES: 4

Corn

Nothing says summer like an ear of corn right off the grill, with some delicious butter spread over it. Grilling corn is simple and foolproof—you just need to start with a good, fresh ear of corn. The ear should be cut off the stalk no more than three days before you eat it. Corn is always the sweetest at the point it's picked. As it ages off of the stalk, it converts sugars to corn starch. Look for ears that have the husk tight around it, with silks that still have some green color on them.

INGREDIENTS

4 ears sweet corn

4 TB. seasoned spreads (see variations)

TOOLS

Bowl filled with ice-cold water for
    soaking corn

Tongs

Serving platter

PREP

1 Medium-High

Preheat the grill to medium-high for direct-heat cooking.

2

In a bowl filled with ice-cold water, soak corn for 15 minutes. For each ear of corn, carefully peel back husk so it's still attached at the base, and remove corn silk. Pull husk back up.

GRILL

1

Using tongs, place corn on the grill over direct heat, and cook for 15 minutes, turning two or three times.

2

Remove corn from the grill and place on a serving platter. Pull back husk on each ear, spread 1 tablespoon seasoned spread, and serve. You can also serve several spreads on the side to allow each guest to choose the one they want.

SEASONED SPREADS

Go beyond butter with any of these delicious spreads for corn:

Mexican Corn: Combine 2 tablespoons mayonnaise, 2 tablespoons plain yogurt, and ½ teaspoon cumin powder. Sprinkle shredded Cotija cheese on top.

Pecan Butter: Combine 4 tablespoons room-temperature butter and 2 tablespoons crushed pecans.

Lime Butter: Combine 4 tablespoons room-temperature butter, 1 teaspoon lime zest, and 1 teaspoon lime juice.

GRILL METHOD:
DIRECT HEAT

PREP TIME:
5 MIN.

COOK TIME:
6-8 MIN.

SERVES: 4

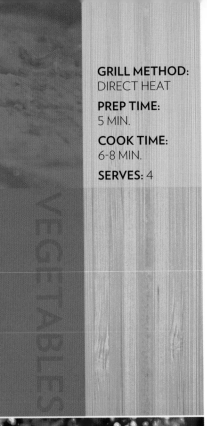

Eggplant

Many people associate eggplant with a certain bitterness, but you can get rid of the bitterness by salting the eggplant and grilling it at a hot temperature. This recipe for eggplant steaks is something you might find in the eastern Mediterranean. You can use a variety of different colors and shapes of eggplant for more visual interest.

INGREDIENTS

1 purple eggplant

2 TB. kosher salt

Vegetable oil

TOOLS

Cutting board

Chef's knife

Transport tray

Tongs

Serving platter

PREP

Medium-High

1 Preheat the grill to medium-high for direct-heat cooking.

2 On a cutting board, cut eggplant into 1-inch-thick (2.5-cm) slices using a chef's knife, season with kosher salt, and allow to sit for 5 minutes. Rub both sides of each slice of eggplant with vegetable oil, and place on a transport tray to take to the grill.

GRILL

1 Using tongs, place eggplant slices on the grill over direct heat, and cook for 2 minutes. Rotate 45 degrees to form the cross-hatch pattern, and cook for 2 more minutes.

2 Flip over eggplant slices, and repeat the process on the other side.

3 Remove eggplant slices from the grill. They should still hold their shape without being totally soft. Arrange eggplant slices on a serving platter and serve.

CHEF'S TIP

When buying eggplant, look for ones that are tight-skinned and firm, and no more than 4 inches (10 cm) wide.

GRILL METHOD
INDIRECT HEAT

PREP TIME:
3 MIN.

COOK TIME:
30 MIN.

SERVES: 4

Garlic

When garlic is roasted on the grill, it tames down those harsh, raw garlic flavors. The individual cloves soften and become a great spread or condiment. Roasted garlic can be used as a spread on sandwiches, from hamburgers, to grilled chicken, to grilled eggplant. This recipe for roasted garlic is very easy to make and stores well. I usually roast several heads at one time, and any I don't use are wrapped in plastic and put in the refrigerator. If you decide to do the same, you can store the garlic for up to a month.

CHEF'S TIP

To eat roasted garlic, squeeze a clove out from the bottom of the bulb, and spread it on bread like butter.

INGREDIENTS

1 head garlic
1 TB. olive oil

TOOLS

Disposable aluminum roasting pan
Cutting board
Chef's knife
Aluminum foil

Tongs
Serving platter

PREP

250°F (121°C)

Preheat the grill to 250°F (121°C) for indirect-heat cooking. Put a disposable aluminum roasting pan under the grate.

On a cutting board, cut top of garlic head off using a chef's knife to expose very top of each of cloves.

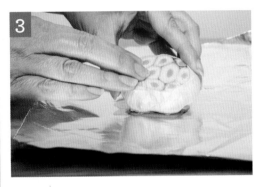

Put garlic head on top of a square of aluminum foil, and rub with olive oil.

Seal garlic in the foil.

GRILL

Using tongs, place garlic on the grill over indirect heat, close the lid, and cook for 30 minutes, maintaining a temperature of 250°F (121°C).

Remove garlic from the grill. Open slowly; steam will roll out as you peel back the foil. Place on a serving platter, and serve.

GRILL METHOD:
DIRECT HEAT

PREP TIME:
10 MIN.

COOK TIME:
20-30 MIN.

SERVES: 4

Lettuce
Caesar Salad

Grilling lettuce seems odd to many people, but you can put romaine on the grill just long enough to give it the grill marks and a little smoky flavor. This recipe pairs it with the tang of Caesar dressing, which is a nice complement to the grilled lettuce. In the end, the heart of the lettuce will still be crispy, and the grilled part will be just slightly wilted. Combining these different textures is pleasing and helps to develop a complete dish. This recipe can be served as a side dish or an entrée.

INGREDIENTS

2 garlic cloves, peeled

3 TB. lemon juice

1 TB. Dijon mustard

2 anchovies (optional)

1 tsp. kosher salt

¼ tsp. black pepper

¾ cup olive oil

½ cup grated Parmesan cheese

2 romaine lettuce hearts

TOOLS

Blender

Serving container

Cutting board

Chef's knife

Transport tray

Tongs

Serving platter

PREP

In a blender, combine garlic, lemon juice, Dijon mustard, anchovies (if using), kosher salt, and black pepper, and pulse a few times to chop up garlic.

Put blender on a high speed, and pour in olive oil in a constant stream.

Pour Caesar dressing mixture into a serving container, and mix in ¼ cup Parmesan cheese by hand.

Remove outer leaves of romaine lettuce, and wash. On a cutting board, cut romaine lettuce hearts in half lengthwise using a chef's knife, and place on a transport tray to take to the grill.

CHEF'S TIP

Lettuces are delicate leaves that, like sponges, will soak up almost any moisture around them to keep the leaves fully hydrated. Be careful to keep them away from things that may produce off flavors in the lettuce by placing them in sealed bags. Also don't put dressing on lettuces until just before serving them. If you put it on too early, the leaves will soak up the acids from the dressing, causing their cell structure to collapse and leaving you with soggy lettuce.

GRILL

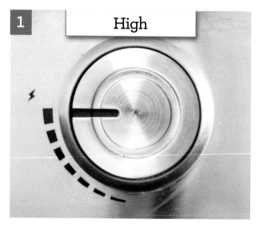

High

Preheat the grill to high for direct-heat cooking.

Using tongs, place romaine lettuce on the grill flat side down over direct heat, and cook for 20 seconds.

Grilled romaine lettuce should have a good grill mark and should be slightly wilted on the outside but still crispy on the inside. Place lettuce on a serving platter with the grill marks up. If it's not going to be served right away, refrigerate.

When ready to serve, drizzle Caesar dressing mixture over romaine halves, being sure grill marks stay visible as you do so. Sprinkle remaining ¼ cup Parmesan cheese over salads, and serve immediately.

GRILLING TRIVIA

Cooking lettuce has a long history dating back to Roman times. A recipe for lettuce and onion soup can be found in early Roman cookbooks, and the father of modern cuisine, Augustus Escoffier, had several recipes for cooked lettuces. Sautéed, braised, fried, or stuffed, lettuce is more versatile than people give it credit for.

THE ORIGIN OF CAESAR SALAD

This salad is said to have been invented by Caesar Cardini in Mexico in 1924. This was during the U.S. Prohibition, when many people traveled to his restaurant to avoid restrictions on alcohol. On a busy day, the restaurant ran short on supplies; acting fast, Caesar looked through the pantry and found the dressing ingredients. He prepared the dressing in the dining room with a flourish, and a classic was born.

GRILL METHOD
DIRECT HEAT

PREP TIME:
20-30 MIN.

COOK TIME:
10 MIN.

SERVES: 4

Mushrooms

For many years, portobello mushrooms have been what chefs have turned to whenever they're serving a vegetarian meal. These mushrooms are big and have a full flavor that will leave you feeling full and happy. Best of all, they're quick and easy to fix. You can use this recipe to cook most varieties of mushrooms; when grilling the smaller species, you can toss them in a grill basket so they don't fall through the grates.

INGREDIENTS

2 garlic cloves, peeled and chopped

3 TB. balsamic vinegar

2 TB. lemon juice

1 TB. dark soy sauce

½ cup dry red wine

1 tsp. dried basil

¼ tsp. black pepper

4 portobello mushrooms

Pan spray

4 TB. bleu cheese

TOOLS

Mixing bowl

Whisk

Soup spoon

Transport tray

Tongs

Serving platter

PREP

1

In a small mixing bowl, whisk together garlic, balsamic vinegar, lemon juice, dark soy sauce, dry red wine, basil, and black pepper using a whisk.

2

Remove stems from portobello mushrooms by carefully holding cap at base of stem in one hand and pulling off stem with your other hand. You can either discard stems or save them to grill with caps. For each mushroom, scrape gills with a soup spoon. Discard gills.

3

Peel mushroom caps by grabbing a piece of flap hanging over the edge and pulling it over top of mushroom.

4

As you pull each flap, you should end up with pie-wedge pieces peeling off each time. Continue peeling around mushrooms.

5

Place mushroom caps on a transport tray gill side up. Pour whisked marinade mixture into caps, and allow to marinate for at least 20 minutes.

GRILL

VEGETABLES

Medium-High

Preheat the grill to medium-high for direct-heat cooking.

Pour any marinade left in mushroom caps back into the mixing bowl. Spray both sides of mushroom caps with pan spray.

Using tongs, place caps over the direct heat cap side down, and allow to cook for 4 minutes.

With the tongs, carefully lift mushroom caps, and pour liquid that has accumulated in them during grilling into the mixing bowl with marinade.

Put caps back on the grill gill side down, and allow to cook for 4 minutes.

Turn over caps, and pour the marinade mixture back in. Top with bleu cheese, and allow to cook with the lid closed for 2 minutes.

Remove mushroom caps from the grill, place on a serving platter, and serve.

CHEF'S TIP

Portobello steaks also make a great burger—just add a bun and your favorite toppings. If you used smaller mushrooms, they are a nice addition to a grilled steak.

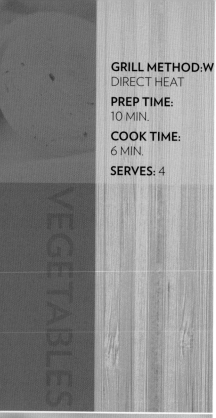

PREP TIME:
10 MIN.

COOK TIME:
6 MIN.

SERVES: 4

VEGETABLES

Onions

Grilled onions are an amazing complement to savory foods. They can be used on steaks and burgers as toppings, included as an ingredient in salsa and other sauces, or eaten on their own as a side dish. Once onions have cooked, they have a sweet character—gone is all the harsh heat of a raw onion. Some people recommend cooking them on aluminum foil so they don't fall through the grate; however, when you do this, you sacrifice the grill flavor. Instead, use a bamboo skewer as suggested in the recipe. That way, you'll end up with a more intense flavor and nice grill marks.

INGREDIENTS

4 large onions

1 TB. kosher salt

1 tsp. black pepper

Pan spray

TOOLS

Cutting board

Chef's knife

Bamboo skewer soaked in water

Transport tray

Tongs

Serving platter

PREP

Preheat the grill to medium-high for direct-heat cooking.

On a cutting board, peel and cut bloom end off of onions using a chef's knife, leaving root end attached.

Slice onion into ½-inch (1.25-cm) slices, and push a bamboo skewer through onion slices to hold rings together.

Season both sides of onions with kosher salt and black pepper, and spray with pan spray.

GRILL

Using tongs, place onions on the grill over direct heat, and cook for 2 minutes. Rotate 90 degrees to form the cross-hatch pattern, and cook for 1 minute.

Flip over onions, and repeat the process on the other side. Remove onions from the grill, place on a serving platter, and serve.

GRILL METHOD:
DIRECT HEAT

PREP TIME:
22 MIN.

COOK TIME:
15–20 MIN.

SERVES: 4

VEGETABLES

Peppers
(Hot and Bell)

Roasted peppers are a common ingredient in many recipes. When peppers are roasted on the grill, they're much more flavorful than when cooked under a home broiler. Once bell peppers are roasted, they can be puréed into a sauce, cut into strips for a burger or steak topping, or even tossed with pasta and olive oil for a great dinner. Roasted hot peppers can be puréed to make a hot sauce that will have you throwing away your shaker of hot sauce in the refrigerator.

CHEF'S TIP

If you roast bell peppers at the same time as hot peppers, the bells will pick up some of the heat. You can do this to add a little element of heat, and then separate out the hot peppers when you're cleaning them.

INGREDIENTS

1 lb. (453.5 g) hot or bell peppers, whole and uncut

Pan spray

TOOLS

Tongs

Plastic zipper-lock bag

Paper towels

Cutting board

Chef's knife

GRILL

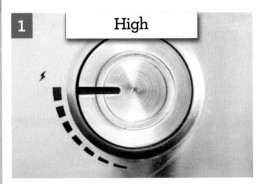

High

Preheat the grill to high for direct-heat cooking.

Spray peppers with pan spray. Using tongs, put peppers on the grill over direct heat. Once bottom sides of peppers are completely black (approximately 5 to 10 minutes), turn peppers to the next side.

As peppers cook, they swell up, causing skin to start to crack away from meat of pepper. Continue to turn peppers as each side turns black, about 5 to 10 minutes, being sure tops and bottoms of peppers are also blackened.

Once peppers are completely black but still pliable, put into a plastic zipper-lock bag, seal, and put in the refrigerator for 20 minutes.

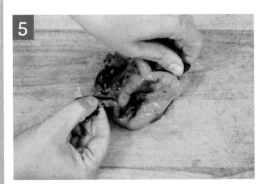

Peppers will be deflated in the bag once cooled. Take out peppers and rub to remove black outer layer.

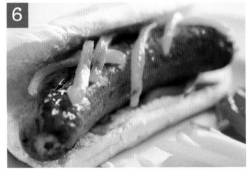

On a cutting board, remove seeds and stems. Using a chef's knife, cut roasted peppers into strips, and use as needed.

GRILL METHOD:
DIRECT HEAT

PREP TIME:
2 MIN.

COOK TIME:
8 MIN.

SERVES: 4

Potatoes

Potatoes can be cooked in many ways. This recipe is a favorite of mine, as slicing the potatoes and cooking them directly on the grill imparts a smoky flavor into the flesh of the potatoes. If you use an Idaho or baking-type potato, they hold together better on the grill. If you use a creamy-style potato (such as redskin or Yukon gold), the texture will be much smoother. But you'll have to watch it a bit more closely, because it can brown quickly. Adding pesto to the potatoes will make them feel more summery with a great herbal character.

CHEF'S TIP

Try to get fresh potatoes, because they have higher water content. As the potato heats up, the water in the potato steams the interior, which is helpful when grilling them.

INGREDIENTS

1 lb. (453.5 g) potatoes of your choice

1 TB. kosher salt

1 tsp. black pepper

Pan spray

½ cup Pesto (see "Seasonings and Condiments")

TOOLS

Cutting board

Chef's knife

Transport tray

Tongs

Mixing bowl

Serving platter

PREP

Preheat the grill to medium for direct-heat cooking.

Rinse off potatoes. On a cutting board, cut into ⅓-inch (.75-cm) slices using a chef's knife. Season with kosher salt and black pepper, spray with pan spray, and place on a transport tray.

GRILL

Using tongs, place potatoes on the grill over direct heat, and cook for 2 minutes. Rotate 90 degrees to form the cross-hatch pattern, and cook for 2 more minutes.

Flip over potatoes, and repeat the process on the other side.

Put potatoes on a serving platter, and spoon on Pesto.

Serve as a side dish along with other grilled items.

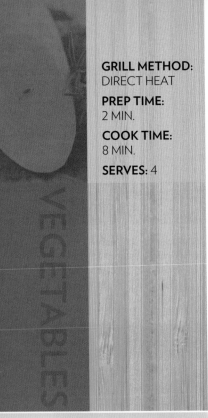

GRILL METHOD:
DIRECT HEAT

PREP TIME:
2 MIN.

COOK TIME:
8 MIN.

SERVES: 4

Summer Squash

Anyone who has grown summer squash in the garden knows they can be prolific. Most gardeners will try to give them away because they can't keep up with the plants. In fact, growing up in the country, the only time my family locked the doors was during squash season—we were scared the neighbors would come in and leave us a table full of them! This recipe is easy yet will make everyone happy, from family members to gourmands. Start with good-quality ingredients, as squash brings out the flavors of whatever it's cooked with.

INGREDIENTS

4 yellow squash, no longer than 6 in.
  (15.25 cm)

1 TB. kosher salt

1 tsp. black pepper

2 cloves garlic, minced

Pan spray

2 TB. balsamic vinegar

TOOLS

Cutting board

Chef's knife

Tongs

Transport tray

Serving platter

PREP

Medium-High

Preheat the grill to medium-high for direct-heat cooking.

On a cutting board, remove stem and bloom ends of yellow squash using a chef's knife. Cut on the bias at a diagonal into ½-inch (1.25-cm) slices, and season with kosher salt and black pepper. Sprinkle slices with garlic, spray with pan spray, and place on a transport tray.

GRILL

Using tongs, place yellow squash on the grill over direct heat, and cook for 2 minutes. Rotate 90 degrees to form the cross-hatch pattern, and cook for 2 minutes.

Flip yellow squash, and repeat the process on the other side.

Remove yellow squash from the grill, and place on a serving platter with your favorite entrée. Drizzle with balsamic vinegar and serve.

SQUASH SIZE AND TASTE

As summer squash grow larger, they develop seeds through the middle. The larger they get, the more bitterness is created from the seed development, so steer clear of the larger summer squash.

GRILL METHOD:
DIRECT HEAT

PREP TIME:
2 MIN.

COOK TIME:
8 MIN.

SERVES: 4

Sweet Potatoes

If I had my way, we'd see a resurgence of this tuber to the levels of the 1920s, when they were eating 29 pounds of them per person each year. Most Americans associate sweet potatoes with the sticky-sweet version served at Thanksgiving. In reality, they are much better if cooked quickly without all the added sugar. Sweet potatoes straight off the grill are a perfect starch accompaniment to most meat dishes. And with a light peach glaze, the traditionalist will get a little bit of sweetness.

INGREDIENTS

1 lb. (453.5 g) sweet potatoes

1 TB. kosher salt

1 tsp. black pepper

Pan spray

½ cup Peach Glaze (see "Seasonings and Condiments")

TOOLS

Cutting board

Chef's knife

Transport tray

Tongs

Mixing bowl

Serving platter

PREP

1 | Medium

Preheat the grill to medium for direct-heat cooking.

2

On a cutting board, peel sweet potatoes and cut into ⅓-inch (.75-cm) slices using a chef's knife. Season with kosher salt and black pepper, spray with pan spray, and place on a transport tray.

GRILL

1

Place sweet potatoes on the grill over direct heat, and cook for 2 minutes. Rotate 90 degrees to form the cross-hatch pattern, and cook for 2 minutes.

2

Flip over sweet potatoes, and repeat the process on the other side.

3

Put sweet potatoes into a medium mixing bowl, add Peach Glaze, and toss. Place sweet potatoes on a serving platter, and serve as a side dish with poultry, pork, or seafood.

SWEET POTATO VARIETIES

There are literally hundreds of varieties of sweet potatoes in many different colors, including red, yellow, white, pink, and orange. Yellow and white ones are lower in sugar than other sweet potatoes. The orange ones are sometimes referred to as yams; however, because they aren't true yams, guidelines in America require that those labeled as yams must also be labeled as sweet potatoes.

GRILL METHOD:
DIRECT HEAT

PREP TIME:
2 MIN.

COOK TIME:
4 MIN.

SERVES: 4

Tomatoes

You might be shocked to hear that tomatoes can be grilled. The grilling process is quick and concentrates the tomato flavor. Grilled tomatoes make a great side dish; you can also chop them up to make salsa or even make a fabulous tomato sauce from them. This recipe is for a side dish. It's great in the morning as a side dish for eggs, because the bright tomato flavor and acids awaken your palate for the day to come. If you don't have time in the morning, try grilling several tomatoes during an evening grill, and then put them in the refrigerator for reheating the next morning. You can sprinkle the grilled tomatoes with some fresh basil for a nice herbal finish.

INGREDIENTS

2 tomatoes

1 TB. kosher salt

1 tsp. black pepper

Pan spray

2 TB. extra-virgin olive oil

TOOLS

Cutting board

Chef's knife

Transport tray

Offset spatula

Serving platter

PREP

Medium

Preheat the grill to medium for direct-heat cooking.

On a cutting board, remove stem end of each tomato, and cut in half from stem end to flower end using a chef's knife. Season with kosher salt and black pepper, spray with pan spray, and place on a transport tray.

GRILL

Using tongs, place tomato halves on the grill cut side down over direct heat, and allow to cook for 4 minutes.

As tomatoes start to soften, skin will loosen from flesh. Remove and discard skin.

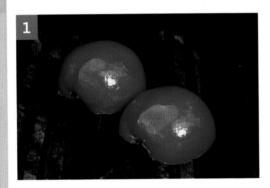

Using an offset spatula, remove tomatoes from the grill and place on a serving platter, being sure tomatoes are grilled side up. Drizzle tomatoes with extra-virgin olive oil and serve as a side dish.

CHEF'S TIP

When picking tomatoes, make sure they were never refrigerated. If tomatoes are put into a temperature below 45°F (7°C), they stop their development. Also, look for tomatoes that are soft to the touch and have red color through the middle when cut open. When in doubt, ask your grocer or vendor.

FRUIT

GRILL METHOD:
DIRECT HEAT

PREP TIME:
5 MIN.

COOK TIME:
8 MIN.

SERVES: 4

FRUIT

Apples

Apples are a fantastic when grilled, with a quality that's especially warming to the soul in the fall and winter. By adding in cinnamon and sugar, as in this recipe, you can really play up that feature. Look for firm apples and ones marked as good "pie apples."

CHEF'S TIP

When buying apples for grilling, try to go directly to an orchard, because fresh ones have a higher water content and aren't coated with anything (such as wax) to preserve them.

INGREDIENTS

2 TB. lemon juice

2 cups water

4 apples

1 TB. granulated sugar

1 tsp. cinnamon

TOOLS

Mixing bowls

Cutting board

Apple corer

Chef's knife

Tongs

Grill basket (optional)

Serving platter

PREP

Preheat the grill to medium for direct-heat cooking.

In a medium mixing bowl, combine lemon juice and water. On a cutting board, core apples with an apple corer, slice into wedges with a chef's knife, and add to the bowl to keep them from turning brown.

GRILL

Remove apples from lemon water, and, using tongs, place on the grill over direct heat. (You may want to use a grill basket to keep apples from falling through the grates.)

Cook apples on one side for 4 minutes. Turn over apples, and repeat the process on the other side.

Remove apples from the grill, and put into a medium mixing bowl. Add sugar and cinnamon while apples are still steaming hot, and toss to coat.

Arrange apples on a serving platter, and serve as a dessert or side dish.

GRILL METHOD:
DIRECT HEAT

PREP TIME:
5 MIN.

COOK TIME:
6 MIN.

SERVES: 4

Apricots

In this recipe, sweet apricots are married with salty prosciutto, an Italian ham that has aged at least 18 months. The burrata cheese also adds texture to the mix. This recipe sets a wonderful tone for a festive evening; in fact, I often serve this as an appetizer with a glass of sparkling Prosecco wine.

INGREDIENTS

2 apricots

4 TB. olive oil

8 slices prosciutto

1 lb. (453.5 g) burrata cheese

TOOLS

Cutting board

Chef's knife

Pastry brush

Tongs

Serving platter

PREP

Preheat the grill to medium-high for direct-heat cooking.

On a cutting board, find ridge line on each apricot, cut into that line, and cut 360 degrees around that point using a chef's knife.

For each apricot, grab sides of apricot, and twist in opposite directions to free pit. Discard seed from middle of each apricot.

Using a pastry brush, brush cut side of apricots with 1 tablespoon olive oil.

GRILL

Using tongs, place apricots on the grill over direct heat, and allow to cook for 3 minutes. Flip over apricots, and repeat the process on the other side.

Remove apricots from the grill, and place on a serving platter. Arrange prosciutto and burrata cheese along the outside of the platter, drizzle remaining 3 tablespoons olive oil over apricots, and serve.

249

GRILL METHOD:
DIRECT HEAT

PREP TIME:
5 MIN.

COOK TIME:
6 MIN.

SERVES: 4

Bananas and Strawberries

Like peanut butter and chocolate, bananas and strawberries are a match made in heaven. A very refreshing dessert in the summertime, this union glows when basked in the heat of the grill. If your kids are big fans of fruit, you can even make a large batch of these and freeze them for a great afternoon frozen treat.

INGREDIENTS

1 TB. honey

4 TB. lime juice

12 strawberries, hulled

2 bananas

TOOLS

Mixing bowl

Small whisk

Cutting board

Chef's knife

Grilling skewers soaked in water

Tongs

Serving platter

PREP

Preheat the grill to medium for direct-heat cooking.

In a medium mixing bowl, whisk together honey and lime juice using a small whisk.

On a cutting board, peel and cut bananas into 1-inch (2.5-cm) round slices using a chef's knife. Add strawberries and banana slices to the bowl, and toss.

Take 4 soaked grilling skewers and thread an equal number of strawberries and bananas on each.

GRILL

Using tongs, place kebabs on the grill over direct heat, and allow to cook for 3 minutes. Flip kebabs, and repeat the process on the other side.

Remove kebabs from the grill, arrange on a serving platter, and serve.

251

GRILL METHOD
DIRECT HEAT

PREP TIME:
5 MIN.

COOK TIME:
4 MIN.

SERVES: 6

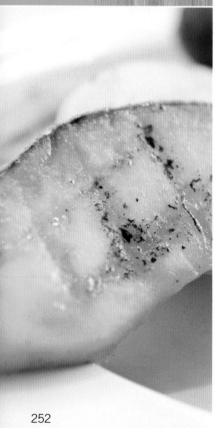

Cantaloupes

Like with most other fruits, grilling cantaloupe is easy and quick. It is fun to see people's faces as you serve this treat for dessert. This recipe also adds a little touch of sweetness with a peach glaze.

CHEF'S TIP

When selecting a melon, look at the stem end. The stem should have been removed cleanly, leaving an indent in the melon where it was. Press the area where the stem was. If you feel a little give in this area, the melon is ripe. If the stem is present or the melon is hard at the stem point, it was picked too early.

INGREDIENTS

1 cantaloupe

1 cup Peach Glaze (see "Seasonings and Condiments")

TOOLS

Cutting board

Chef's knife

Tongs

Pastry brush

Serving platter

PREP

Preheat the grill to medium-high for direct-heat cooking.

Rinse cantaloupe under cold running water. On a cutting board, cut off stem end about 1 inch (2.5 cm) from the end using a chef's knife. Do the same thing on bloom end, and discard cut-off pieces.

Cut cantaloupe in half from end to end, remove seeds, and slice into half rings about 1 inch (2.5 cm) thick.

GRILL

Using tongs, place cantaloupe slices on the grill over direct heat, and allow to cook for 2 minutes. Flip over cantaloupe, and repeat the process on the other side.

Remove cantaloupe from the grill, and brush meat of cantaloupe with Peach Glaze using a pastry brush. Arrange cantaloupe slices on a serving platter, add any leftover Peach Glaze for dipping, and serve.

PREP TIME:
5 MIN.

COOK TIME:
4 MIN.

SERVES: 4

FRUIT

Mangoes

This recipe combines mango and strawberry sauce, creating a symphony of sweetness. Serve it with a scoop of ice cream or frozen yogurt for a decadent treat.

CHEF'S TIP

If you want to save some time and energy trying to figure out where the seed is in the fruit, you can use a mango cutter. This tool looks somewhat like an apple corer/slicer and is used to help cut down around the mango seed.

INGREDIENTS

2 mangoes
4 TB. olive oil
4 oz. strawberry sauce

TOOLS

Cutting board
Chef's knife
Pastry brush
Tongs
Serving platter

PREP

Preheat the grill to medium-high for direct-heat cooking.

On a cutting board, cut off stem end of mangoes about ½ inch (1.25 cm) from end using a chef's knife. Do the same thing on bloom end, and discard cut-off pieces. Working your way around each mango, cut off skin.

Standing each mango on end, cut through center, following around large seed. Do this a second time, going around other side of seed.

Using a pastry brush, brush mango fruit pulp with 1 tablespoon of olive oil per half.

GRILL

Using tongs, place mangoes on the grill over direct heat, and allow to cook for 2 minutes. Flip over mangoes, and cook for 2 minutes.

Cut the mango into ½-inch (1.25-cm) dice. Place on a serving plater, top with strawberry sauce, and serve.

255

GRILL METHOD:
DIRECT HEAT

PREP TIME:
5 MIN.

COOK TIME:
8 MIN.

SERVES: 4

FRUIT

Oranges

Orange is the world's favorite flavor, after chocolate and vanilla. And their flavor is even more interesting when you grill them. This recipe uses an orange-flavored liqueur to intensify the orange flavor and help with caramelization. You can leave the peel on for this recipe, as the bitterness from the peel is offset by the sugars developed during the grilling process.

INGREDIENTS

2 oranges

4 TB. Grand Marnier

TOOLS

Cutting board

Chef's knife

Pastry brush

Tongs

Serving dishes

PREP

Medium-High

Preheat the grill to medium-high for direct-heat cooking.

On a cutting board, slice oranges into ½-inch (1.25-cm) slices using a chef's knife. Remove any seeds that are visible, and, using a pastry brush, brush both sides of orange slices with Grand Marnier.

GRILL

Using tongs, place oranges on the grill over direct heat, and allow to cook for 2 minutes. Rotate oranges 90 degrees, and allow to cook for 2 minutes to form the cross-hatch pattern.

Flip over oranges, and repeat the process on the other side.

Serve orange slices on top of your favorite entrée

CHEF'S TIP

Grilled orange slices are a great accompaniment to fish dishes.

GRILL METHOD
DIRECT HEAT

PREP TIME:
5 MIN.

COOK TIME:
12 MIN.

SERVES: 4

Peaches

This recipe unites the rich grilled flavors of peaches with the sweet tastiness of marshmallows. Peaches should have a slight give to them without being mushy. When buying peaches for grilling, look for freestone varieties, because the pit will easily come out of them.

GRILLING TRIVIA

Peaches were originally cultivated in Ch as early as 1000 B.C.E. Peach blossoms a sacred plant there, as they are a symbol immortality and unity.

INGREDIENTS

2 peaches
4 TB. amaretto
4 marshmallows

TOOLS

Cutting board
Paring knife
Pastry brush
Tongs
Serving platter

PREP

Preheat the grill to medium for direct-heat cooking.

On a cutting board, find ridge line on each peach, cut into that line, and cut 360 degrees around that point using a paring knife.

For each peach, grabbing sides of peach, twist in opposite directions to free pit. Discard seed from middle of peach.

Using a pastry brush, brush cut surface of peach halves with amaretto.

GRILL

Using tongs, place peaches cut side down on the grill over direct heat, and allow to cook for 4 minutes.

Move peaches to a cooler area of the grill with the cut side up, and place 1 marshmallow on top of each half. Close the grill lid, and allow peaches to cook for 8 minutes. Remove peaches from the grill, arrange on a serving platter, and serve.

GRILL METHOD
DIRECT HEAT

PREP TIME:
5 MIN.

COOK TIME:
8 MIN.

SERVES: 4

Pears

Pears are often an overlooked fruit. That's too bad, because they have such a great sugar-acid balance that's really pleasing to the palate. In this recipe, you develop a real richness to the pears by caramelizing some of the sugars and add another layer of flavor with soft goat cheese scooped on top. This can stand alone as a vegetarian entrée or can be a great side dish for pork. No matter what you use it for, this dish is an easy way to make people think you're a grill master chef.

INGREDIENTS

2 pears

1 TB. sea salt

1 tsp. ground pink peppercorns

2 TB. olive oil

¼ lb. (113.5 g) soft goat cheese

TOOLS

Cutting board

Chef's knife

Melon baller

Pastry brush

Tongs

Serving platter

PREP

Medium

Preheat the grill to medium for direct-heat cooking.

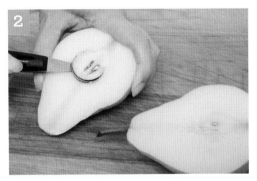

On a cutting board, cut pears in half from stem end to base using a chef's knife. Scoop out pear seeds using a melon baller.

Season cut side of pears with sea salt and pink peppercorns, and brush all over with olive oil using a pastry brush.

GRILL

Using tongs, place pears cut side down on the grill over direct heat, and allow to cook for 4 minutes. Rotate pears 90 degrees to form the cross-hatch pattern, and allow to cook for 4 minutes.

Remove pears from the grill, and immediately place goat cheese in the depression where seeds were. You may need to cut a little off curved side of each pear to help it sit flat. Arrange pears on a serving platter, and serve as a main course, dessert, or side dish.

GRILL METHOD
DIRECT HEAT

PREP TIME:
10 MIN.

COOK TIME:
8 MIN.

SERVES: 6

FRUIT

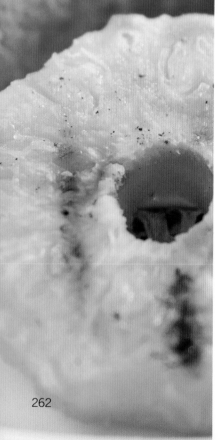

Pineapples

Pineapple is one of the few fruits that continues to mature after it's picked from the tree, so this is a dish you could make any time of year and still be able to find high-quality pineapples. This recipe is a grilled version of Pineapple Madagascar, with the caramelized sugars from the pineapple producing a mouthwatering butterscotch flavor. This simple and quick yet elegant and exciting-to-eat delicacy is sure to impress your guests.

INGREDIENTS

1 fresh pineapple

4 TB. white rum

8 TB. orange juice

TOOLS

Cutting board

Chef's knife

Apple corer

Mixing bowl

Tongs

Ice-cream scoop

Serving platter

PREP

Preheat the grill to medium for direct-heat cooking.

On a cutting board using a chef's knife, cut off top of pineapple about ½ inch (1.25 cm) below leaves. Cut off bottom of pineapple about ½ inch (1.25 cm) above the bottom, and cut off outside, going just below the eyes.

Slice pineapple into ¾-inch (2-cm) slices. Using an apple corer, cut out center of each slice. In a medium mixing bowl, combine white rum and orange juice. Add pineapple slices, and toss.

GRILL

Using tongs, place pineapple slices on the grill over direct heat, and allow to cook for 2 minutes. Rotate pineapple slices 90 degrees, and allow to cook for 2 minutes. Flip pineapple slices, and repeat on the other side.

Remove pineapple from the grill. Place on a serving platter, and serve as a side dish or with ice cream as a dessert.

GRILL METHOD
DIRECT HEAT

PREP TIME:
5 MIN.

COOK TIME:
6 MIN.

SERVES: 10

FRUIT

Watermelon

This recipe combines watermelon with the tangy flavors of balsamic vinegar and feta cheese into a salad. You could also use the grilled watermelon as an ingredient in other things, such as a watermelon salsa, or as a side dish all by itself.

CHEF'S TIP

Watermelon is 90 percent water (go figure), which may make some people wonder whether grilling will make it soft or soggy. By grilling it at a higher heat, just long enough for the grill marks to appear, the watermelon should maintain its structure. In the end, it should be slightly dehydrated on the outside but firm in the middle of each slice.

INGREDIENTS

1 (about 6 ½–lb. [about 3–kg]) water-melon

3 TB. sea salt

1 TB. black pepper, coarsely ground

10 oz. (283.5 g) feta cheese, cubed ½ in. (1.25 cm)

10 TB. balsamic vinegar

TOOLS

Cutting boards

Chef's knives

Tongs

Serving platter

PREP

Medium-High

Preheat the grill to medium-high for direct-heat cooking.

On a cutting board, cut off top of watermelon about 1 inch (2.5 cm) below the stem using a chef's knife. Cut off bottom bloom end about 1 inch (2.5 cm) above bottom, and cut off outside rind, exposing pink flesh. Slice watermelon into ¾-inch (2-cm) slices, and season with sea salt and black pepper.

GRILL

Using tongs, place watermelon slices on the grill over direct heat, and allow to cook for 2 minutes. Rotate watermelon slices 90 degrees, and allow to cook for 2 minutes to form the cross-hatch pattern.

Flip over watermelon slices, and cook for 2 minutes to form the cross-hatch pattern on the other side.

Remove watermelon slices to a clean cutting board, and cut into 2-inch cubes using a chef's knife. Remove any visible seeds.

Toss watermelon with feta cheese cubes, and drizzle with balsamic vinegar. Place on a serving platter, and serve as a side dish or a standalone salad.

265

BREAD/
CHEESE

GRILL METHOD:
DIRECT HEAT

PREP TIME:
2 MIN.

COOK TIME:
4 MIN.

SERVES: 10

Pita Bread

In the Middle East, almost everything is served with warm pita bread. When you're grilling out, this is a great bread to serve. It's a small bite that people can nibble on with hors d'oeuvres and eat with entrées. I like this with things from grilled cheeses to steaks. It could also be used for the bread of a grilled burger.

INGREDIENTS

5 pita rounds

2 TB. extra-virgin olive oil

1 tsp. garlic salt

TOOLS

Pastry brush

Tongs

Cutting board

Chef's knife

Basket or plate (to hold pita bread)

PREP

Preheat the grill to high for direct-heat cooking.

Brush pita bread with extra-virgin olive oil using a pastry brush, and season with garlic salt.

GRILL

Using tongs, place pita bread on the grill, and cook for 2 minutes.

Flip pita bread, and cook for 2 minutes. It may puff up; this is normal.

Remove pita bread from the grill to a cutting board, and cut each piece into 4 wedges with a chef's knife.

Arrange pita bread in a basket. Additional serving suggestions including pairing with grilled vegetables, hummus, or grilled lamb, or just enjoying pita bread by itself.

GRILL METHOD:
DIRECT HEAT

PREP TIME:
5 MIN.

COOK TIME:
8 MIN.

SERVES: 4

Garlic Bread

Instead of plain bread with dinner, you can dress it up easily with this recipe for garlic bread. Garlic can burn if you put pieces directly on the bread and then put it on the flames, and it can be really strong if you just mince it up and put it on after it's cooked. To tame the heat of the garlic and keep it from burning, you're going to rub it onto the grilled bread.

GRILLING TRIVIA

In northeast Spain, this style of garlic bread is served with tomato pressed into it. To do this, cut a plum tomato in half and rub it into the bread after you rub in the garlic.

INGREDIENTS

1 loaf crusty French bread

½ cup extra-virgin olive oil

8 cloves garlic, peeled

TOOLS

Cutting board

Serrated knife

Pastry brush

Tongs

Serving platter

PREP

Preheat the grill to medium for direct-heat cooking.

On a cutting board, cut French bread on the bias into 1-inch (2.5-cm) slices using a serrated knife. Using a pastry brush, brush both sides of bread with extra-virgin olive oil.

GRILL

Using tongs, place bread on the grill over direct heat, and cook for 2 minutes. Rotate bread 90 degrees to form the cross-hatch pattern, and allow to cook for 2 minutes.

Flip bread, and repeat the process on the other side.

Remove bread from the grill. Take a whole clove of garlic and rub it onto all parts of grilled bread.

Arrange garlic bread on a serving platter, and serve.

GRILL METHOD:
DIRECT HEAT

PREP TIME:
30 MIN. + 3 HR.

COOK TIME:
10-16 MIN/PIZZA

SERVES: 10

Pizza

Pizza is a worldwide favorite. Many families have pizza night, where they make their own pizzas and try to create the perfect pizza pie. Top the crust in this recipe with your favorite toppings and start a new family tradition.

CHEF'S TIP

If I'm making pizza for a get-together, I partially cook several pizza crusts before the guests arrive at my house. That way, each person can add their toppings, and all I need to do is finish cooking the pizza. Any unused partially cooked pizza crusts can be frozen for up to 3 months.

INGREDIENTS

4 lb. (1.75 kg) pizza dough
Assorted pizza toppings

TOOLS

Rolling pin
Rimless cookie sheet
Cutting board
Chef's knife
Serving platters

PREP

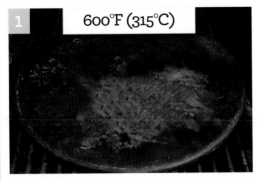

600°F (315°C)

With the pizza stone on it, preheat the grill to 600°F (315°C) for indirect-heat cooking; in this case, you will have the heat on below the pizza stone as well.

For each pizza, roll out about 5 ounces of dough so it's 1 inch (1.25 cm) thick.

GRILL

Using a rimless cookie sheet, place dough on the preheated stone, and allow to cook with the lid closed for 4 minutes.

Remove partially cooked pizza crust from the grill. Turn over, and top with assorted pizza toppings.

Put pizza back on the hot pizza stone, and place the lid back on the grill. Allow pizza to cook until top is toasted to your liking, about 6 to 12 minutes.

Remove pizza to a cutting board, and cut into wedges with a chef's knife. Place pizzas on a serving platter, and serve.

GRILL METHOD:
DIRECT HEAT

PREP TIME:
5 MIN.

COOK TIME:
6 MIN./QUESADILLA

SERVES: 4

Tortilla Quesadilla

Quesadillas are a wonderful expression of Americanized Mexican food. What most Americans think of as a quesadilla is a flour tortilla–grilled cheese sandwich cut into wedges. In reality, this is called something completely different in Mexico. In this recipe, I give a nod to the true Mexican version with melted, stringy cheese in corn tortillas folded in half. The flavor of the grill blends with the toasted corn tortillas to give the quesadillas a nice, nutty flavor.

INGREDIENTS

8 corn tortillas

1 lb. (454 g) Oaxaca cheese

1 cup Salsa Verde (see "Seasonings and Condiments")

TOOLS

Pizza stone

Tongs

Serving platter

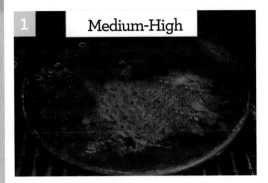

Medium-High

With the pizza stone on top, preheat the grill to medium-high for direct-heat cooking.

For each quesadilla, using tongs, place 1 corn tortilla on the pizza stone, and arrange about 2 ounces (57 grams) Oaxaca cheese on top.

When cheese melts, about 6 minutes, fold tortilla over to form a half circle.

Remove quesadilla from the grill, arrange on a serving platter with Salsa Verde on the side, and serve.

COOKING QUESADILLAS

If you don't have a pizza stone, you can do this in a cast-iron skillet on the grill. The true Mexican cooking pan that quesadillas are cooked in is called a *comal*. It looks like a cast-iron skillet without sides.

GRILL METHOD
DIRECT HEAT

PREP TIME:
5 MIN.

COOK TIME:
6 MIN.

SERVES: 4

Halloumi Cheese

Halloumi is the cheese that most Westerners know as the cheese in saganaki—the flaming cheese at Greek restaurants. This cheese is similar to fresh mozzarella in that it's formed and shaped in hot water. This means it has an extremely high melting point, so you can cook it directly on your grill and it won't melt. Halloumi is salty, making it nice to pair with things that contrast with that saltiness, such as the acid in lemon or the sweetness of a sweet wine. It's also low in acid, so this recipe has you add acid by way of grilled lemons.

INGREDIENTS

1 lb. (454 g) halloumi cheese

1 lemon

4 leaves mint

2 TB. olive oil

TOOLS

Cutting board

Chef's knife

Pastry brush

Tongs

Serving platter

PREP

Preheat the grill to medium-high for direct-heat cooking.

On a cutting board, cut halloumi cheese into strips 2 inches (5 cm) wide, slice lemon into ½-inch (1.25-cm) wheels, and chop mint leaves using a chef's knife.

GRILL

Using a pastry brush, brush cheese and lemon wheels with olive oil. Using tongs, place them on the grill over direct heat.

Cook cheese and lemon wheels for 2 minutes. Rotate cheese and lemon wheels 90 degrees to form the cross-hatch pattern, and cook for 1 minute.

Flip cheese and lemon wheels, and repeat the process on the other side.

Remove from the grill, and arrange on a serving platter, alternating cheese and lemon wheels. Top with mint, and serve.

GRILL METHOD:
INDIRECT HEAT

PREP TIME:
15 MIN.

COOK TIME:
18-20 MIN.

SERVES: 8

Corn Bread

Corn bread and grilling naturally go together. But in the heat of the summer, nobody wants to heat up the oven in the house. So why not make the corn bread on the grill? If you cook other things on direct heat at the same time as you cook the corn bread, it will pick up the yummy grill flavors.

INGREDIENTS

2 cups cornmeal

2 tsp. baking powder

2 tsp. granulated sugar

¼ tsp. table salt

1 large egg, beaten

1 ½ cups buttermilk

5 TB. butter, melted

2 TB. vegetable oil

TOOLS

12-in. (30.5-cm) cast-iron skillet

Mixing bowls

Whisk

Toothpick

Butter knife

Dinner plate

Chef's knife

PREP

Preheat the grill to 400°F (204°C) for indirect-heat cooking. Place a 12-inch (30.5-cm) cast-iron skillet on the grill to preheat at the same time.

In a large mixing bowl, combine cornmeal, baking powder, sugar, and table salt. In a small bowl, mix together beaten egg, buttermilk, and melted butter with a whisk.

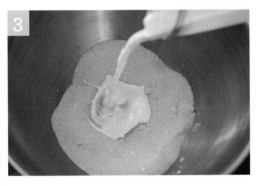

Make a well in dry ingredients in the large mixing bowl, and pour wet ingredients into the well. Don't overmix; it should be a lumpy mixture.

Oil the inside of the cast-iron skillet with vegetable oil.

CHEF'S TIP

Corn bread is classified as a "quick bread." Quick breads use baking powder or baking soda as leaveners, so the minute the wet and dry ingredients are mixed, they start to bubble up. Because of this, you must start cooking the batter as soon as it is mixed. If you hesitate, you'll end up with a hard, dense corn bread.

Pour corn bread mixture into the cast-iron skillet, close the lid, and allow to cook for 18 minutes.

Check the doneness of corn bread by sticking a wooden toothpick in the middle. If it comes out clean, it's ready to come off the grill. If there's batter stuck to the toothpick, allow corn bread to cook for another 2 minutes.

Remove cast-iron skillet from the grill, and run a butter knife around the edge of the skillet between corn bread and lip of the pan. Place a dinner plate upside down on top of the skillet, and quickly flip together so the plate is facing up and the skillet is upside down.

Cut corn bread into wedges with a chef's knife, and serve hot.

VARIATIONS OF CORN BREAD

Corn bread was invented out of necessity when English settlers arrived in the Americas. The settlers learned that wheat was not being grown in North America yet, so Native Americans taught them how to use corn, which was a foreign grain to the Europeans. The settlers adapted corn to fit into their recipes.

Corn pone: Made from a thick cornmeal batter that doesn't have eggs or milk in it and fried in an iron pan.

Hot-water corn bread: The batter is made with boiling water and self-rising cornmeal and is fried on the stovetop into 3- to 4-inch (7.5- to 10-cm) pieces.

Hushpuppies: A thick batter made with cornmeal and buttermilk. The batter is fried in oil to make small round balls of cornmeal.

Johnnycakes: Thin cornmeal batter. These are cooked into what look like pancakes.

GRILL METHOD:
DIRECT HEAT

PREP TIME:
15 MIN.+ 3 HR.

COOK TIME:
3 MIN.

SERVES: 4

BREAD/
CHEESE

Brick Sandwiches

This recipe uses the concept of compressing the sandwich, but it also warms everything on the grill. This melts the cheese and helps to marry all the flavors together. Combining the pesto and tomatoes with the cheese gives the sandwich the flavor of a caprese salad. This is a great middle-of-the-summer recipe, when tomatoes are fresh and the smell of basil flavors the markets.

INGREDIENTS

1 loaf Italian bread

2 tomatoes, sliced

1 TB. sea salt

4 TB. Pesto sauce (see "Seasonings and Condiments")

1 cup Parmesan cheese, grated

Pan spray

TOOLS

Bricks

Aluminum foil

Cutting board

Chef's knife

Parchment paper or waxed paper

Serving platter

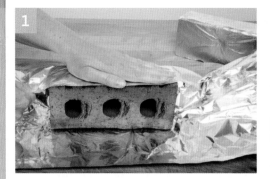

Wrap 4 bricks individually in aluminum foil.

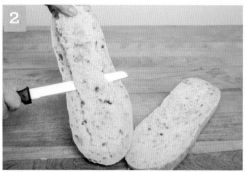

On a cutting board, slice Italian bread in half lengthwise with a chef's knife, and scoop out center of loaf. Sprinkle tomato slices with sea salt.

Spread pesto sauce on both halves of bread. Layer salted tomatoes and sprinkle Parmesan cheese on bottom half of bread.

Wrap sandwich in parchment paper, and lay bricks across the top. Allow sandwich to sit at room temperature for at least 3 hours.

Medium-High

Preheat the grill to medium-high for direct-heat cooking. Remove bricks and parchment paper from sandwich, and place bricks on the grill. Spray outside of sandwich with pan spray. Place sandwiches on the grill over direct heat, put a hot brick on top of each, and cook for 1 minute.

Flip over sandwiches, and repeat the process. Remove sandwiches from the grill, place on a serving platter, and serve warm.

283

DESSERTS

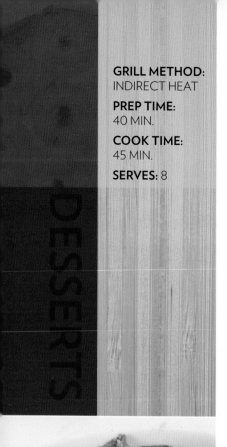

GRILL METHOD:
INDIRECT HEAT

PREP TIME:
40 MIN.

COOK TIME:
45 MIN.

SERVES: 8

Pineapple Upside-Down Cake

With this pineapple upside-down cake, you get a rustic outdoor feeling by using an iron skillet. Cooking upside-down cake in the skillet also helps develop the mouthwatering brown caramel topping around the pineapple rings.

INGREDIENTS

2 cups cake flour

2 tsp. baking powder

¼ tsp. iodized salt

3 eggs, separated

1 tsp. vanilla extract

1 cup whole milk

¾ cup butter

1 ½ cups granulated sugar

1 cup dark brown sugar

1 (20-oz. [567-g]) can pineapple rings

14 maraschino cherries

TOOLS

12-in. (30.5-cm) cast-iron skillet

Mixing bowls

Stand mixer or hand mixer

Rubber spatula

Whisk

Wooden toothpick

Hot pads

Butter knife

Serving platter

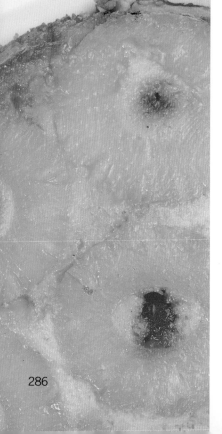

PREP

350°F (177°C)

Place the cast-iron skillet on the grill. Preheat the grill to 350°F (177°C) for indirect-heat cooking.

In a medium mixing bowl, combine cake flour, baking powder, and iodized salt using a rubber spatula.

Using a mixer, whip egg whites into stiff peaks. Set aside. In a large mixing bowl, combine vanilla extract and whole milk using a whisk.

In a stand mixer, or using a hand mixer and mixing bowl, cream together ½ cup butter and granulated sugar on high speed until combined and creamy looking. Add egg yolks one at a time, waiting for each to be fully mixed in before adding the next one.

Turn the mixer down to a low speed, and add ⅛ of dry ingredient mixture to creamed mixture. When that's fully mixed, add ⅛ of vanilla-milk mixture. Keep alternating until batter is fully mixed.

Using the rubber spatula, fold egg whites delicately into batter by hand.

DESSERTS

Place remaining ¼ cup butter and dark brown sugar into the hot cast-iron skillet on the grill, and mix, evenly coating the bottom of the skillet with the mixture.

Add pineapple rings and maraschino cherries to the skillet.

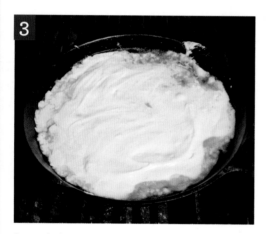

Pour cake batter into the skillet.

Cook cake for 45 minutes. Test for doneness by sticking a wooden toothpick into the center of the cake. If it comes out clean, it's ready. If there's a bit of a batter on the toothpick, close the lid and allow to cook for a few more minutes.

Remove the skillet from the grill with hot pads. Run a butter knife around the inside of the skillet to make sure cake isn't sticking to the sides of the skillet.

While the skillet is still hot, place a serving platter upside down on top of the skillet, centered over cake. Quickly flip the skillet with the platter so cake comes out onto the platter. Remove the skillet.

Serve cake.

GRILL METHOD:
INDIRECT HEAT

PREP TIME:
40 MIN.

COOK TIME:
30 MIN.

SERVES: 8

Fruit Pie

After you're done cooking all your meats and the grill is cooling down, you can cook a rustic fruit pie. As everyone is eating dinner, the pie can be baking. Then, once everyone's finished, you can serve an amazing pie from the grill while it's still warm. Use your imagination for the filling; almost any fruit that's in season will work. For this recipe, I use strawberries.

INGREDIENTS

2 cups all-purpose flour

1 tsp. iodized salt

⅔ cup vegetable shortening

5 TB. ice-cold water

1 tsp. white vinegar

2 ⅔ cups strawberries, sliced

¼ cup granulated sugar

1 TB. cornstarch

4 TB. milk, any kind

TOOLS

Mixing bowls

Rubber spatula

Pie pan

Parchment paper

Butter knives

Rolling pin

Cake pan

Pastry brush

Hot pads

PREP

If you're using a premade pie crust, skip to Grill 1.

In a small mixing bowl, combine all-purpose flour and iodized salt using a rubber spatula. Place the bowl and vegetable shortening in the refrigerator to chill for 15 minutes.

Place a pie pan upside down on top of a sheet of parchment paper, and draw a line on the paper around the outside of the pan.

Remove flour-salt mixture and vegetable shortening from fridge. Cut vegetable shortening into flour-salt mixture using 2 butter knives in a scissors motion; it should be lumpy at this point. Add ice-cold water and white vinegar, and stir.

Form dough into 2 even-size balls. Add a little flour to the parchment paper, and roll out dough balls to the size of the ring you drew on the paper with a rolling pin.

In one of the pie crusts, cut a 2-inch (5-cm) ring out of middle.

Place other crust into the pie pan.

GRILL

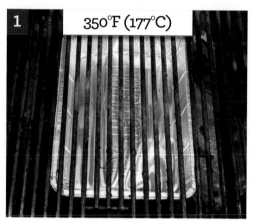

1 350°F (177°C)

Preheat the grill to 350°F (177°C) for indirect-heat cooking.

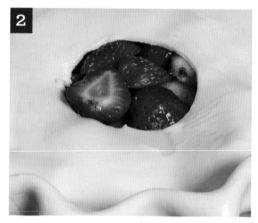

2

In a medium bowl, combine strawberries, sugar, and cornstarch. Pour mixture into the crust-lined pie pan. Place top crust so hole is centered on pie, and crimp edges together.

3

Using a pastry brush, brush top crust with milk.

4

On the grill, place an empty cake pan upside down. Place the pie pan on top of the cake pan, and bake for 30 minutes, or until crust is golden brown and delicious and fruit is bubbling.

5

Remove pie from the grill with hot pads, and allow to rest for 30 minutes. Serve.

CHEF'S TIP

The pie-crust dough should stay cold as you're making it. If it warms up before you roll it out, it will become tough. Also, make sure little bits of the vegetable shortening are scattered through the crust, as this will produce a light, flaky crust.

GRILLING TRIVIA

Pies have a long history of being cooked over the fire. The first pies appeared in 9500 B.C.E. When war parties would travel they would often make hearty pies to sustain them on the journeys. Even sailors would make and store their pies for overseas travel. In medieval times, the use of ovens was taxed because of the cost of building them, so people would make pies over the fire instead of paying additional fees.

GRILL METHOD:
INDIRECT HEAT

PREP TIME:
15 MIN.

COOK TIME:
20 MIN.

SERVES: 8

Peach Cobbler

A great outdoor dessert, this super-easy cobbler delivers peach flavors with a crunchy granola topping. You can add a scoop of ice cream to the top of this for a cool treat on a hot day. For an adult version, you can also add a splash of your favorite bourbon to the peach mixture. For added grilled flavor, you can grill the peaches before putting them in the cobbler. If you do this, reduce the overall cooking time to 15 minutes.

INGREDIENTS

1 tsp. ground cinnamon

½ cup melted butter

6 freestone peaches

½ cup light brown sugar

⅔ cup granola

TOOLS

Mixing bowls

Paring knife

Cast-iron Dutch oven *or* 8-in. (20.25-cm) cake pan

Rubber spatula

Hot pads

Serving bowls

PREP

Preheat the grill to 350°F (177°C) for indirect-heat cooking.

In a small mixing bowl, combine cinnamon and melted butter.

For each freestone peach, find ridge. Following ridge, cut all the way around peach to pit using a paring knife, and twist peach halves to separate peach from pit.

Cut each peach half into 4 wedges, and place in a medium mixing bowl. Add ¼ cup butter-cinnamon mixture and ¼ cup light brown sugar, and toss.

In a medium mixing bowl, combine granola, remaining butter-cinnamon mixture, and remaining ¼ cup brown sugar with a rubber spatula. The mixture should be somewhat dry and clumpy, like a streusel topping.

In a room-temperature, cast-iron Dutch oven, place peaches. Sprinkle granola mixture over top of peaches.

GRILL

20 minutes

Place the Dutch oven on the preheated grill. Put the lid back on top of the grill.

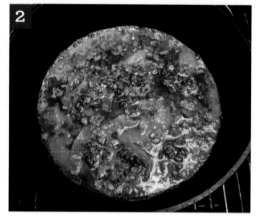

Allow cobbler to bake for 20 minutes, or until topping is browned and peaches are bubbling.

Remove cobbler from the grill using hot pads, and allow to rest for 30 minutes. Scoop cobbler into serving bowls, and serve with a scoop of ice cream or splash of bourbon.

GRILLING TRIVIA

Cobbler originated in the U.S. colonies. Colonists were short on ingredients to make a traditional English suet pie, so they patchworked together dough to top their dish. The rest is history.

COBBLERS BY ANOTHER NAME

Cobblers have many different names around the world. They are all a combination of a sweet or savory ingredient with a biscuit or scone crust. Some names that you might know include the Betty, grump, dump, slump, or sonker. The crisp or crumble adds an oatmeal layer. Grunts, pandowdy, and slumps are made on the stovetop. A buckle is made with more of a cakelike batter.

GRILL METHOD:
INDIRECT HEAT
PREP TIME:
30 MIN.
COOK TIME:
10 MIN.
SERVES: 6

DESSERTS

Chocolate Lava Cakes

This extremely rich and decadent dessert is a chocolate lover's dream come true. I challenge anyone to be able to eat a portion without a tall glass of milk. You can even serve these little cakes with fresh cherries and ice cream for added dimension.

INGREDIENTS

6 oz. (170 g) bittersweet chocolate

2 oz. (56.75 g) semisweet chocolate

10 TB. butter

½ cup all-purpose flour

1 ½ cups confectioners' sugar

3 eggs

3 egg yolks

1 tsp. vanilla extract

2 TB. cherry liqueur

Pan spray

TOOLS

Pizza stone

Microwave-safe mixing bowl

Rubber spatula

Mixing bowls

Whisk

6-oz. (170-g) ramekins

Hot pads

Butter knife

Serving plates

PREP

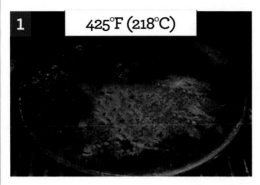

1 425°F (218°C)

Preheat the grill and a pizza stone to 425°F (218°C) for indirect-heat cooking.

2

In a medium microwave-safe bowl, place bittersweet chocolate, semisweet chocolate, and butter, and put in the microwave for 15 seconds at 50 percent power. Mix chocolate using a rubber spatula, return to the microwave, and continue heating and mixing until mixture is completely melted and incorporated together.

3

In a small mixing bowl, combine all-purpose flour and confectioners' sugar, and add to chocolate-butter mixture.

4

In a small mixing bowl, lightly whisk together eggs and egg yolks with a whisk. Add to rest of batter, and mix.

5

Add vanilla extract and cherry liqueur, and mix.

6

Spray the inside of 6 ramekins with pan spray. Divide batter evenly among the ramekins.

GRILL

Place the ramekins on top of the pizza stone, and cover immediately with the grill lid to conserve heat.

10 minutes

Cook for 10 minutes, or until outside of cakes are fully set and centers are still a little soft. Remove the ramekins from the grill using hot pads.

Run a butter knife between the ramekins and cakes all the way around.

For each cake, put a serving plate upside down on top of cake. Flip ramekin and plate at the same time.

Lift the ramekin so that cake is left on the plate for serving. Serve cakes while still piping hot.

CHEF'S TIP

This recipe requires mastery of your grill, because the temperature needs to be dialed in very close to 425°F (218°C) and stay consistent. If you overcook the cake, the "lava" becomes a brownie; if you undercook the cake, it will fall apart when you turn it out. However, it's definitely worth the experimentation.

GRILL METHOD:
DIRECT HEAT

PREP TIME:
3 MIN.

COOK TIME:
3 MIN.

SERVES: 6

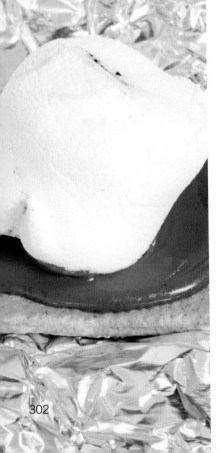

S'mores

S'mores are a campfire classic. Here, instead of toasting the marshmallow over the open flame, you fully assemble the s'mores before cooking them. This allows the chocolate to melt and the marshmallows to cook without catching on fire and falling off the stick. Once you get used to grilling them, try getting more creative with s'mores by using cookies instead of graham crackers or adding a slice of grilled fruit to the sandwich. I also like to add mint or basil to the mix to give the s'mores a unique flavor.

INGREDIENTS

6 graham crackers

6 marshmallows

6 squares milk chocolate

TOOLS

Aluminum foil

GRILL

Preheat the grill to medium-high for direct-heat cooking.

For each s'more, on a sheet of aluminum foil, layer ½ graham cracker, 1 square of chocolate, 1 marshmallow, and top with ½ graham cracker.

Loosely seal the foil. Place s'mores on the grill, and cook for 3 minutes.

Remove s'mores from the grill, take off aluminum foil, and serve.

GRILLING TRIVIA

While s'mores don't have a verified origin, the first printed record of a s'mores recipe was in the Girl Scouts manual *Tramping and Trailing with the Girl Scouts* in 1927.

GRILL METHOD:
DIRECT HEAT

PREP TIME:
1 MIN.

COOK TIME:
2 MIN.

SERVES: 6

Donuts

Timing the trip to the donut shop correctly is the ultimate in dining experiences. When you walk into the shop, you can smell the donuts cooking and the coffee brewing. Then, when you bite into the just-cooked warm donut you ordered, it melts away in your mouth. This recipe duplicates that warm-donut experience and enables you to make day-old donuts taste fresh again. You can even try this grilling technique with other types of pastries as well.

INGREDIENTS

6 glazed yeast donuts

TOOLS

Offset spatula

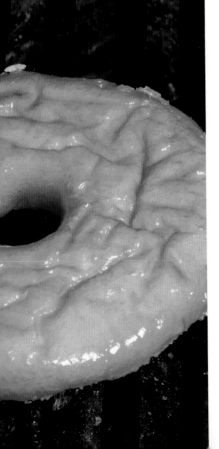

GRILL

Preheat the grill to medium-high for direct-heat cooking.

Cut donuts in half horizontally.

Place unglazed sides on the grill, and cook for 1 minute.

Flip donuts, and cook for 1 minute. Remove donuts from the grill with the offset spatula, and serve.

CHEF'S TIP

Using donuts as sandwich buns has become a trend spurred on by carnivals. To do this, you can put the meat of the sandwich on the glazed sides of each half and have the unglazed sides face out at the top and bottom. This works particularly well with pork or chicken dishes, as the sweetness accents the meat.

INDEX

INDEX

INDEX

INDEX